IMAGES
of America

ROCKY HILL
KINGSTON AND GRIGGSTOWN

The Delaware and Raritan Canal languidly snakes through the lovely Millstone River Valley landscape of central New Jersey. On this stretch of the main canal between Kingston and Rocky Hill there were barges, steamboats, and yachts at various times during its commercial period. A railroad spur connected the two villages with the main line between New York and Philadelphia at Monmouth Junction. Today, the Delaware and Raritan Canal State Park maintains pathways on both sides of the canal along this stretch for recreational purposes.

IMAGES
of America

ROCKY HILL
KINGSTON AND
GRIGGSTOWN

Jeanette K. Muser

ARCADIA

Published by Arcadia Publishing,
an imprint of Tempus Publishing, Inc.
2 Cumberland Street
Charleston, SC 29401

Printed in Great Britain.

Library of Congress Catalog Card Number: 98-87569

For all general information contact Arcadia Publishing at:
Telephone 843-853-2070
Fax 843-853-0044
E-Mail arcadia@charleston.net

For customer service and orders:
Toll-Free 1-888-313-BOOK

Visit us on the internet at http://www.arcadiaimages.com

This book is dedicated to my husband, Rainer Karl Martin Muser, and my two children, Frederick Josef Moehn and Juliette Marie Moehn.

CONTENTS

ACKNOWLEDGMENTS

Preparing this book has fulfilled a personal goal and also the need to write the story of these three villages on the Millstone River and the Delaware and Raritan Canal. From the outset of this project, it was evident that the people who live here were enthusiastic and supportive of such a book. Gathering the images and the information was one of the most rewarding experiences I have ever had and it is to all of these wonderful people that I am indebted. Special thanks to members of the Griggstown Historical Society, the Kingston Historical Society, the Rocky Hill Community Group and volunteers, Margaret Carlsen of Rockingham, and James Amon of the Delaware and Raritan Canal Commission. I am particularly grateful to John Auciello, chief ranger of the Delaware and Raritan Canal State Park, for his help with the history of the canal; Martha Strunsky, Lou Sincak, George Luck Jr., and Rick Goeke of Kingston; John Allen, Lloyd Staats, Lloyd Van Doren, George Rightmire, Virginia Dey Craig, Esther Olsen, Raymond and Evelyn Peters, Virginia Skillman, Kay Langeland, Shirley Staats Stryker, and Henry Lasch of Griggstown; Raymond Whitlock Jr., Nancy Nicholson, Lloyd Lewis, Vivian Engelbrecht, Ted Merritt, Peggy Harris, Carl Robbins, and Constance Greiff of Rocky Hill; Diane Sliney of Blawenburg; Bob Yuell of Plainsboro; Ursula Brecknell of Belle Mead; and Sally Davidson of Princeton for their expertise and help.

Photographs were loaned by all of the above organizations and by many individuals. Sources for other photographs were the Historical Society of Princeton, Princeton University Library, and Rutgers University Library. Throughout the book, credit to the owner of the photograph will be given. Images without a credit are in the Rocky Hill Community Group archives. I am also grateful for the expert reproductive photographic printing done by Sam and Kim at Triangle Copy Center in Rocky Hill.

Published sources that were valuable for general information are *Millstone Valley* by Elizabeth G.C. Menzies, *New Jersey and the Revolutionary War* by Alfred Hoyt Bill, *The Rockingham Story* by Elizabeth Bates Carrick, *Episodes in the History of Griggstown* by Laura P. Terhune, *Rocky Hill, New Jersey: 1701–1964* by Vivian F. Engelbrecht, *Memoirs of Rocky Hill* by Thayer A. Bolmer, *Along the Delaware and Raritan Canal* by James and Margaret Cawley, *The Delaware and Raritan Canal: a History* by Crawford Clark Madeira Jr., *The Delaware and Raritan Canal: a Pictorial History* by William J. McKelvey Jr., the *Jersey Midlands* by Henry Charlton Beck, *The Old Copper Mines of New Jersey* by Harry B. Weiss and Grace M. Weiss, and articles from the New Jersey Historical Society journals and *Princeton History* published by the Historical Society of Princeton.

INTRODUCTION

The villages of Rocky Hill, Kingston, and Griggstown in the Millstone River Valley are known to most people today because of troop movements through this area during the Revolutionary War and Gen. George Washington's stay at "Rockingham" near Rocky Hill in 1783 while the Continental Congress was in session in Princeton. It was here that Washington wrote his "Farewell Orders to the Armies of the United States." However, the fertile river valley drew settlers long before these historic events. Lenni Lenape Indians left numerous trails for travellers, northern European land speculators, and farmers to find their way into this area of New Jersey. Dutch, French Huguenot, English, and Scottish names soon appeared as the area developed during the Colonial period. Gristmills and fulling mills were built to process the wheat and the flax and wool produced on the farms.

Commercial ventures followed soon after agriculture was established. The copper mine in Griggstown attracted Welsh miners before the Revolution. Copper ore had to be hauled and shipped to England for treatment. Roads were poor and difficult to travel at the time. The idea of a canal across the "waistline" of New Jersey to connect Philadelphia and New York had been discussed long before 1830, when the construction of the Delaware and Raritan Canal began. The Rocky Hill Railroad and Transportation Company built a spur from Kingston that extended to the Atlantic Terra Cotta factory between Rocky Hill and Griggstown. Freight of various kinds was transported by waterway and railway at the same time that roads began to improve.

As more people moved into the villages, merchants were attracted and new general stores opened in all three towns. Taverns and inns were a part of every village. Kingston developed as a transportation center being on the "post road" stagecoach route between Trenton and New Brunswick and being the mid-point on the Delaware and Raritan Canal. Griggstown remained rural. Along with the commercial boom came the need for building new homes, establishing schools and churches, and planning community events to bring people together during leisure times. Soon, regular village events such as baseball games, swimming, fund-raisers, and plays defined the quality of life. For more than three hundred years, Rocky Hill, Kingston, and Griggstown have shared a common historical, commercial, and cultural heritage.

Kingston's historic four-arch stone bridge over the Millstone River is a reminder of earlier times, when General Washington's troops passed through after the Battle of Princeton in January 1777 and when stagecoaches brought passengers and post between Philadelphia and New York during the 19th century. A footbridge over the river existed before 1702 and was improved in 1738. The stone bridge replaced the earlier bridges. A milestone marker embedded in the present stone bridge reads, "Kingston Bridge-1793-Phil. 45 M-N.Y. 50 M." The bridge is now part of the Kingston Mill Historic District in Princeton Township, which is adjacent to the Delaware and Raritan Canal State Park. (Courtesy of Lou Sincak.)

One

WHEN WASHINGTON WAS HERE

Gen. George Washington occupied Rockingham from August 23 until November 9, 1783. John Berrien had purchased the 130-acre farm in the 1730s. To accommodate his growing family, Berrien enlarged the house, bought more land, and renamed his house Rockingham. Also known as "Washington's Headquarters," preservation efforts and the State of New Jersey have saved the house as Rockingham Historic Site. This photograph, taken in the late 19th century, shows the front of Rockingham as the house appeared on its original site on the east side of the Millstone River. (Courtesy of Rockingham Historic Site.)

The Revolutionary War Period

Rocky Hill is known to most people today because of George Washington's headquarters called Rockingham. The house is now a New Jersey State Historic Site and is one reminder of the Revolutionary War period in the villages of Rocky Hill, Kingston, and Griggstown in the lower Millstone River Valley.

Gen. George Washington was at Rockingham while he participated in the Continental Congress at Nassau Hall in Princeton in 1783. The roads, bridges, farms, mills, and taverns that Washington probably saw as he rode on horseback to and from Princeton need to be imagined today as they perhaps appeared over two hundred years ago.

While General Washington was staying at Rockingham, he frequently visited the nearby Van Horne farm, which was located south of today's Route 518 between the village center of Rocky Hill and Route 206. John and Phebe Van Horne were the first of the Van Horne family to occupy the more than 1,000 acres. The Van Hornes had also invited the young New Jersey artist William Dunlap to stay with them during that autumn of 1783. The 17-year-old Dunlap had lost the use of an eye in a childhood accident but his artistic inclinations continued to grow. Arrangements were made for General Washington to pose for a portrait.

Many guests were invited to Rockingham during Washington's three-month stay in Rocky Hill. Among the guests was political pamphleteer, Thomas Paine, whose second pamphlet *The Crisis* had spirited the troops just before the Battle of Princeton in early 1777. Paine and Washington went out in a boat on the Millstone River near the milldam to do an experiment with the "swamp gas." Paine later delivered a speech in 1806 claiming that there was a connection between swamp gas and yellow fever.

Shortly before Washington left Rockingham in November, he issued his "Farewell Orders to the Armies of the United States." What is believed to have been his study is now one of the restored colonial rooms in the house.

Going back one hundred years before Washington lived in Rocky Hill, it is believed that by 1683 Henry Greenland had a house and tavern on the old Lenni Lenape Indian trail that passed through present-day Kingston. Greenland's daughter married Daniel Brinson and their son, Barefoot Brinson, inherited the 300-acre property and built a gristmill sometime before 1748, when Brinson died. Jacob Skillman was the second person to operate a mill on the property, but it was burned by the British in 1776.

In 1797, Major John Gulick and his brother Jacob rebuilt the mill and sublet part of it for a fulling mill and a sawmill. The bridge over the Millstone River, which had been destroyed after the Battle of Princeton, was rebuilt in stone in 1793. The Gulicks developed a section of the Old Post Road as the Kingston and Princeton Branch Turnpike in 1807, which enabled their stage line to compete with others using the "straight turnpike," which is now Route 1. The Greenland-Brinson-Skillman-Gulick House, the gristmill, and the stone four-arch bridge are now part of the Kingston Mill Historic District, which today is part of Princeton Township.

After the Battle of Princeton on January 3, 1777, Washington and his troops marched on the Old Post Road to Kingston where the General conducted his famous "conference on horseback" on the hill at the cemetery. He and his officers decided to head towards Rocky Hill and Griggstown for winter quarters in Morristown rather than continue to New Brunswick where the British had a major supply cache. Washington was back in Kingston and Rocky Hill again in June 1778 on route to the Battle of Monmouth.

The path of Washington's continental troop march north to Morristown is noted on a plaque in Griggstown on the old Somerset Court House Road (now Canal Road). "By this route, Washington and his army retired after his victory at Princeton, January 1777." Benjamin Skillman and his son, Thomas B. Skillman, ran the Black Horse Tavern along this road until 1809 when they lost their license for harboring the "ruffscruffs of the country." The Red Horse Tavern was part of the Colonial William Beekman farm a bit farther south on the road.

Scots-Irishman John Honeyman moved to Griggstown in 1776 and was considered a Tory by the locals during the Revolution. Masquerading as a loyalist butcher behind British lines, he allegedly secretly supplied Washington with valuable information. Some say that Honeyman was the model for James Fenimore Cooper's Harvey Birch in his novel, *The Spy*.

Gen. George Washington personally commanded only five military events during the Revolution. Three of these were fought in New Jersey. Continental troops moved through the Millstone River Valley after the battles of Trenton and Princeton, and before the Battle of Monmouth. By 1781, France had solidified an alliance with America. Comte de Rochambeau's French troops marched through Griggstown and Rocky Hill to Princeton. Rochambeau's troops saw the mills at Rocky Hill that had been purchased in 1773 by John Hart, a signer of the Declaration of Independence. Washington sent a letter to Rochambeau from Chatham on August 28, 1781, stating: "I shall not have the honor of joining your Excellency till we arrive at Princeton . . . " Plans were made to secretly shift the armies to Virginia in preparation for the Battle of Yorktown. When the French marched northward in September 1782 after the Battle of Yorktown, Lauzun's Legion, commanded by Colonel Dillon, camped in the Kingston area to protect the New Brunswick road from possible British attack from New York.

John Berrien was one of the first members of his French-Huguenot family to move to New Jersey. He was appointed a Somerset County judge in 1739 and later served in the New Jersey Assembly. In 1764, Berrien was chosen as a judge in the New Jersey Supreme Court, and he was a trustee of the College of New Jersey (now Princeton University) from 1762 until 1772. It is said that Berrien drowned himself in the Millstone River on April 21, 1772, the day he made his will. (Courtesy of Rockingham Historic Site.)

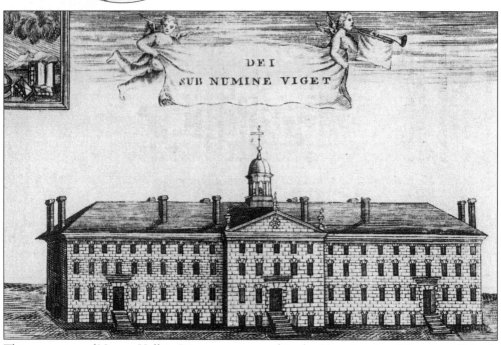

This engraving of Nassau Hall in Princeton appeared in the *New American Magazine* of March 1760. The College of New Jersey offered the use of Nassau Hall for the Continental Congress to meet. The Congress convened in Princeton on June 30, 1783 with 22 delegates. Washington was summoned to participate and arrived at Rockingham in August. (Courtesy of Princeton University Library.)

This portrait of George Washington was done by the young New Jersey painter William Dunlap while the General was staying at Rockingham. Dunlap was a guest of John and Phebe Van Horne of Rocky Hill and Washington was a friend and frequent visitor at the Van Horne house. He agreed to pose for Dunlap's pastel on paper. The young artist also completed a full-length portrait of the General on the battlefield at Princeton. Dunlap's father was so impressed by his son's artistic promise that he sent him to London the following year to study under Benjamin West. Dunlap may not be considered as a major American artist today, but throughout his lifetime he was regarded as a competent painter. (Courtesy of the Architect of the Capitol, Washington, D.C.)

The old milldam at Rocky Hill was close to the Hart-Polhemus mills (page 18). It was here that Thomas Paine and George Washington conducted their scientific experiment to observe the nature of "swamp gas." On a scow in the Millstone River, Paine asked the soldiers to use a pole to disturb the water while he and Washington lit cartridge paper and watched the flame descend to the water's surface.

Both Thomas Paine and George Washington were interested in what caused diseases and how diseases spread. Epidemics of small pox, yellow fever, and cholera were common. Paine concluded from the swamp gas experiment that such vapors did exist in sluggish waters and that yellow fever was caused by miasmas, or swamp gas. It was actually methane gas that bubbled to the surface. This engraving of Thomas Paine is by W. Sharp. (Courtesy of the New York Historical Society.)

What is believed to be George Washington's study at Rockingham was called at one time the "Blue Room." It was here that the General's "Farewell Orders to the Armies of the United States" was put on paper. This upstairs room is in the oldest part of the original Berrien house. (Courtesy of the Historical Society of Princeton.)

Washington's "Farewell Orders to the Armies of the United States" was transcribed into the orderly book of the day on November 2, 1783 and simultaneously published in various newspapers in the colonies. The "Orders" were also read at West Point. (Courtesy of the Library of Congress, Washington, D.C.)

The oldest part of the Greenland-Brinson-Gulick house is believed to have been built by Henry Greenland in 1683 in what was then part of the village of Kingston. The house and mill had deteriorated by 1755 when Jacob Skillman bought the property. He built a second gristmill at the approximate site of the present mill. Major John Gulick bought the farm between 1790 and 1793. The property passed to his son, John Gulick Jr., in 1828, and later to a grandson of Major John Gulick. (Courtesy of the Historical Society of Princeton.)

The mill was burned by the British in December 1776, and the bridge was destroyed by General Washington's troops to delay the British retreat from the Battle of Princeton in January 1777. The bridge was rebuilt in 1798 and is the only remaining four-arch stone bridge in central New Jersey. (Courtesy of the Delaware and Raritan Canal Commission.)

John Honeyman's house in Griggstown may still be seen on Canal Road. During the Revolution, he was thought to be a British spy by the locals, but evidently, he was secretly supplying Washington with information. On December 20, 1776, it is said that Honeyman took note of the British-Hessian position at Trenton by driving cattle in the area and passed his observations along to Washington. His legendary role as Washington's spy has never been conclusively proven.

A portion of the cellar in the Skillman house in Griggstown along the Millstone River was the Black Horse Tavern during the Revolutionary War. The Marquis de Chastellux traveled in America and passed through Griggstown in November 1780 stopping at the Black Horse Tavern, which the Frenchman described as "an indifferent inn but kept by obliging people." (Courtesy of Virginia Skillman.)

17

The Hart-Polhemus gristmill in Rocky Hill pictured here was bought in 1773 by John Hart of Hopewell. Robert Lettis Hooper had previously owned the property and by 1747 had added a fulling mill and dye house to the mill complex. Hart formed a partnership with his son-in-law, John Polhemus, and they continued to operate both mills. Hart's son Jesse managed the transportation of the flour, feed, and textiles. Although a yeoman farmer with only a meager education, John Hart stood beside Adams, Jefferson, and Franklin at the Continental Congress of 1776 and was a signer of the Declaration of Independence. After the Battle of Princeton in January 1777, British soldiers attempted to destroy the bridge and Hart's mill at Rocky Hill, but Col. Daniel Morgan's riflemen with a cannon saved the day. The gristmill was demolished in 1935.

Two

THE DEVIL'S FEATHER BED

This detail from an engraving of Howell's Quarries about 1872 shows the terrain around Rocky Hill. Rockingham can be seen on top of the hill, and the Rocky Hill bridge tender's house is on the left. (Courtesy of Rockingham Historic Site.)

"A Very Difficult and Rocky Hill"

Early travelers through the Millstone River Valley, called the "Mattawong River" by the Native Americans, used old Native American pathways and primitive roads to explore and record what they saw. As early as 1679, Jasper Dankers and Peter Sluyter noted the terrain around Rocky Hill. As the Dutchmen journeyed toward today's Trenton, on what is probably now Mount Lucas Road, they recorded in their journal a "very difficult and rocky hill" near what is now the village of Rocky Hill.

Less than ten years later, Henry Greenland built a house and a tavern on the river at Kingston. Several other land speculators purchased large tracts in the Rocky Hill-Kingston-Griggstown area. By 1735, there were several large property owners in the valley. We have already heard the names Berrien and Van Horne in Rocky Hill. The Harrisons ran the first gristmill in Rocky Hill and Peter Vanderveer bought 500 acres from the Skillmans on the west side of the river. The Higgins family from Massachusetts owned a large tract between today's Route 27 in Kingston and Route 518 through Rocky Hill, and the Gulicks bought along the river. The Griggs brothers and the Veghte family were among the first settlers of Griggstown followed soon by Abraham Van Voorhees, Christyaen Van Doren, Christopher Hoagland, and Hendrik Cortelyou.

Peter Kalm, the early Swedish professor, botanist, and traveler, mentioned the area around Rocky Hill in 1748 in his journal, "Travels." Kalm wrote, "This morning we proceeded on our journey (from Princeton) . . . on a hill covered with trees and called Rockhill. I saw several pieces of stone or rock so big that they would have required three men to roll them down."

John Stevens Sr. came to America in 1699 and heard accounts of copper mines discovered in the "Devil's Feather Bed" near Rocky Hill. He purchased various pieces of land including the Rocky Hill mine, but he died in 1737 and the mine passed to his son, John Stevens Jr. The *Pennsylvania Gazette* of January 16, 1753, ran a news item that stated, "We hear from Rocky Hill in the Jersies that a valuable copper vein of Six Foot Square, is very lately found there." Little more is heard about the mine until 1755, when Stevens attracted investors in the Rocky Hill mine. John Stevens Jr. had become a member of the New Jersey Assembly and was later to be president of the 1787 convention that ratified the Constitution. Robert Hunter Morris, a chief justice in New Jersey and later governor of Pennsylvania, and Elias Boudinot, who later played a prominent role in the Continental Congress in Princeton, were among those who saw the potential of the copper mine in 1755. Several men formed a partnership. The land surrounding the mine was purchased from Abraham Polhemus and a stamping mill was built to crush the ore for shipment to New Brunswick and then on to England for treatment. The mine was a financial failure by 1764, and it was put up for sale and reopened again in 1765 with 160 Welsh miners. Mining ceased when the Revolutionary War broke out, and the property remained idle until 1826, when the Franklin Copper Mining Company reopened the mines. In 1848, stocks were issued and the name was changed to the Rocky Hill Mining and Manufacturing Company. By 1866, the mine was again a failure.

In 1901, two investors attempted to reopen the mine, and finally the New Jersey Copper Company used better equipment and began copper-mining operations again in 1905. The operation continued to flounder until 1916 when the mine was pumped out and reopened because copper prices were up and copper stocks were a favorite among speculators. All mining ceased a few months later. Copper Mine Farm and Copper Mine Road in Griggstown today are reminders of those many years.

"*The Travellers Directory: or, A Pocket Companion, shewing the Course of the Main Road from Philadelphia to New York; and from Philadelphia to Washington . . .*" issued in 1804, provides a glimpse of road conditions at the end of the 18th century. For example, "Rocky Hill, commonly called 'The Devil's Feather Bed,' was formerly very difficult and dangerous to pass, from the great numbers of massy stones promiscuously distributed on the surface; but, the state having directed the repairs of public roads, this has received its share of improvement, and is now made much more convenient and easy to travellers."

This rough terrain referred to above is Ten Mile Run Mountain on the east side of the Millstone River. This diabase and shale geologic structure was soon to be discovered by commercial ventures. The hill was being quarried before 1869, when David H. Mount purchased over 100 acres, including Washington's headquarters called Rockingham, and expanded the Rocky Hill Quarry Company on a portion of the property. He transferred title to the quarry portion of the land and Rockingham to Martin A. Howell of New Brunswick in 1872. Howell's Quarries operated at that time when road and railroad construction required crushed stone. Opportunities for skilled workers from Italy drew new immigrants to the area. This was the "transportation age," when improvements were the order of the day. The Delaware and Raritan Canal and the Pennsylvania Railroad next to the quarry provided for the transport of crushed stone during this period.

At this time Rockingham was being used by the quarry manager, and later it became a boardinghouse for the Italian workmen. However, during all of this, what is believed to be Washington's study was kept neat and orderly out of respect for the first president. The decline of the old house came to the attention of Miss Kate McFarlane of Rocky Hill, who was determined to save Rockingham. During 1896, she solicited funding from private sources and the house was purchased from the quarry and moved up the hill. Rockingham was first opened to the public in 1897—although not completely furnished.

The New Jersey Industrial Directory of 1909 lists the Delaware River Quarry Company of Rocky Hill as having three hundred employees, 250 of them being Italians. Operations of the quarry declined steadily until 1918 when it closed. In 1930, the business was reopened by Theodore Potts. Linus R. Gilbert purchased the quarry in 1933 and renamed it the Kingston Trap Rock Quarry. Mr. Gilbert was very involved in the community of Rocky Hill and built a swimming pool on River Road and a recreational center in the basement of Voorhees Hall.

Quarry operations continued to encroach on Rockingham, and in 1956, Mr. Gilbert agreed to move the house a second time. Cooperation between the historical preservation interests of various groups, the Delaware and Raritan Canal environmental and recreational interests, and the commercial interests of Trap Rock Industries of Kingston has now resulted in an agreement to move Rockingham again in the year 2000 and to preserve the house for posterity.

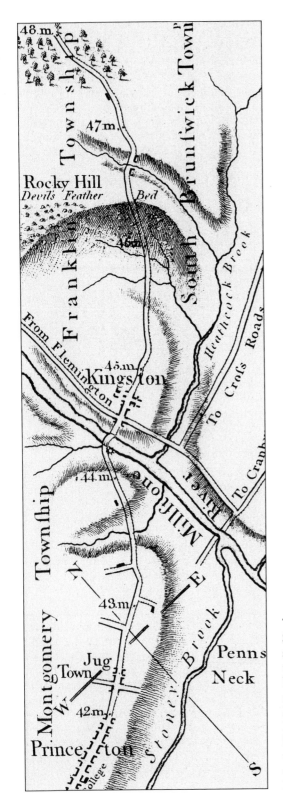

This 1804 map, based on a survey done by S.S. Moore and T.W. Jones, originally appeared in "*The Traveller's Directory . . .*" that provided details about road travel between Philadelphia and New York. The map has been reprinted in *New Jersey Road Maps of the 18th Century*. The name, "The Devil's Feather Bed," as shown on this map, had originated nearly one hundred years earlier when the copper mine was operating during the Colonial period. (Courtesy of the Princeton University Library.)

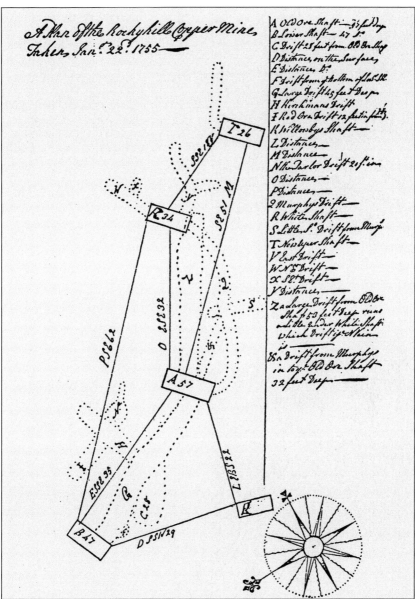

John Stevens Jr. was successful in attracting investors in the Rocky Hill copper mine. Robert Hunter Morris became one of the partners in 1755. Morris asked for a plan of the mine and ore samples for a London assayer to evaluate. At this time, Morris became the governor of Pennsylvania for a brief time before returning to his position as a chief justice in New Jersey. This map details early plans and offered hope for future profits. A stamping mill to separate the ore was next to Nicholas Veghte's gristmill in Griggstown and both were probably run by the same waterpower. During the time when Richard Stevens was the mine manager, Elias Boudinot prepared a description of an ore-roasting oven that he thought would benefit the Rocky Hill operation. However, soon the *Pennsylvania Gazette* of November 15, 1764, carried a notice that the mine was for sale. Welsh miners worked the mine for another few years until the Revolution. (Courtesy of the Morris Family Papers at Rutgers University Library.)

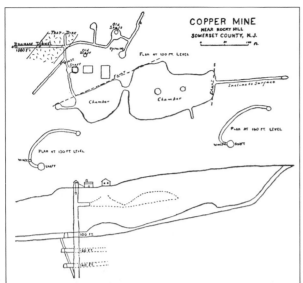

This plan of the copper mine at Rocky Hill-Griggstown appeared in a 1905 prospectus of the New Jersey Copper Company. The main ore mineral was chalocite with small amounts of native copper, which is not of a high grade. From 1900 to 1905, the owners of the Rocky Hill mine reported that on the basis of numerous assays, workable quantities of gold and silver were present in their mine. This claim was later contradicted by a geological survey done by the state. This map was reprinted in the 1906 annual report of the New Jersey State Geologist. (Courtesy of the Historical Society of Princeton.)

The New Jersey Copper Company opened the mine between Rocky Hill and Griggstown in 1905 with improved equipment. New processes were highlighted to attract investors, and many speculators lost money on these ventures. The mine property covered 152 acres between the Millstone River and hill. The drain tunnel was 1,600 feet long. By this time ore was being transported to the Newark and Jersey City smelting centers. (Courtesy of the Historical Society of Princeton.)

This photograph of the canal where the Old Georgetown Road meets Canal Road in Franklin Township now belongs to Traprock Industries Inc. of Kingston. This spot had been an important waterway crossing since 1716, when the Old Georgetown Road was built. An 1860 map shows D.H. Mount owning the structure on the left and a nearby storehouse at the Rocky Hill boat turning basin. Daniel Mount bought adjacent quarry property in 1869. An 1873 map shows J.G. Stryker as owning the house and a lumber business on part of the property. This photograph was probably taken in the early 20th century when the hill in the foreground was fondly called "Mutton Hill" for all its sheep grazing.

This photograph of the quarry loading dock between Kingston and Rocky Hill shows conveyors loading stone products into canal boats in the Delaware and Raritan Canal. The canal boat on the left is unloaded and rests higher in the water. Notice the towpath on the left and the railroad tracks in the foreground. This photograph probably dates from the early 20th century.

This engraving, done around 1872, is a composite of the many activities going on at the Delaware and Raritan Canal during the height of canal freight operations. Martin A. Howell operated the quarry at that time. Note the mules and driver on the towpath hauling canal boats

Early quarry workers dealt with many obstacles in their efforts to produce the stone needed for industrial and transportation purposes.

ROCKY HILL, N. J.

ES STONE LAND.
AD OR CANAL.
WICK, N. J.

TOOL HOUSE.

STONE BREAKER.

CRUSHED STONE
FOR RIAL ROAD BALLAST,
WALKS, GARDEN PATHS, CONCRETE FOUNDATION
STREETS AND AVENUES.

in the direction of Kingston. The obelisk markers on the towpath indicate mileage along the canal.

Quarry operations in the diabase hills drew immigrant workers primarily from Italy. Some of these skilled stone masons also found work with building projects at Princeton University, road construction, canal maintenance, and many other local projects. (Courtesy of the Historical Society of Princeton.)

Horse, wagon, and shovel were replaced with derricks, cranes, trucks, and other modern quarry equipment as the company grew and expanded after 1930. The quarry still operates today on the Delaware and Raritan Canal between Rocky Hill and Kingston as Traprock Industries Inc. of Kingston. An interpretive site of quarry and canal history has been developed at the Rocky Hill bridge over Route 518. (Courtesy of the Brian family of Kingston.)

The Delaware River Quarry Company of Rocky Hill owned 24 small steam engines to transport crushed stone by rail. After 1871, the Pennsylvania Railroad operated this railroad spur. Longtime Kingston residents remember how the conductors of the trains had to swing a lantern at the Kingston crossing on Route 27 to warn drivers. This rail connection was discontinued in the early 1970s.

Three

ROADWAYS, RAILWAYS, AND WATERWAYS

Rarely do researchers find an exact date for an old photograph, but this postcard image has the date of July 19, 1923, written on the back. This view of Route 518 at the Rocky Hill swing bridge, bridge tender's house, and railroad station illustrates the importance of various forms of transportation to this crossroads village. Note the old telephone poles with glass insulators prized today as paperweights. The Georgetown-Franklin Pike, which is now called Route 518, was constructed in 1820 to connect New Brunswick on the Raritan River with Lambertville on the Delaware River.

Transportation Connections

The old Lenni Lenape Indian meandering footpaths that led Dutch settlers to the Millstone River Valley became the early roads and postal routes. As the English gained influence in the colonies, New York and Philadelphia became the leading colonial cities in the mid-Atlantic region. Because the ocean route was impractical, commerce developed between the two cities and roads needed to be improved to handle stagecoaches instead of the individual horse and rider. The Old Georgetown Road connecting New Brunswick with Rocky Hill continuing on Leonard's cartway (now Mount Lucas Road) to Princeton was complete by 1716. This was used primarily by farmers at that time. Up until 1700, no regular passenger vehicles operated along the New York-Philadelphia route through Kingston, although some sort of a road existed as early as 1702. Innkeepers were the first unofficial postmasters. The "stagecoach era" began in 1737 on the road through Kingston between Trenton and New Brunswick called the "King's Highway." This road became the connection between Philadelphia and New York. Stages usually had four horses, and competition for passengers and freight developed. John Mersereau's "Flying Machine" was mentioned in 1765 as the fastest stage service on this route. It took about two days for the trip and four changes of horses. Horses were changed every 15 miles, making this distance a "stage" in the journey.

Roads were measured in "rods" by surveyors. The old Somerset Road through Griggstown and Rocky Hill established in 1723, was sometimes called "The Four Rod Road." That would have been 5.5 yards wide. This road was widened in 1744 and River Road from Rocky Hill to Kingston on the west side of the river was improved that same year. The road from Kingston to Rocky Hill (now Laurel Avenue) on the east side of the river, which connected with the old Somerset Road, was laid out in 1740.

To encourage more travel, inns and taverns along the major roads proliferated. An ideal location for a tavern was on a road at a bridge over a stream or river, where coachmen would change horses or poor weather conditions caused delays. Kingston, Rocky Hill, and Griggstown in the Millstone River Valley were early rest stops for travellers. These early rugged roads, however, did not satisfy the growing commerce in central New Jersey. The first third of the 19th century was the "turnpike era," when various methods of raising money for improved roads were tried. The Old Post Road, or "King's Highway," ceased to be the main route after the "straight turnpike" (Route 1) was completed in 1804. After the King's Highway was improved in 1807 by John Gulick and others, the road was then called the Princeton and Kingston Branch Turnpike. This alternate route (now Route 27) carried land traffic into Princeton to what is now Mercer Street and the Princeton Pike. Turnpike traffic did not, however, increase as rapidly as expected.

The War of 1812 and the British blockade of the coast drew the attention of businessmen who saw the need for a waterway connecting the Delaware River with the tidewater of the Raritan Bay at New Brunswick. This would create an inland waterway to connect Philadelphia and New York City. Ocean travel was dangerous and required about two weeks. Good roads were still hard to find. In 1830, the New Jersey Legislature granted a charter to the Delaware and Raritan Canal and Banking Company and another charter to the Camden & Amboy Railroad and Transportation Company. Both companies began construction and in 1831, the New Jersey Legislature adopted the "Marriage Act," which joined the two companies.

Canal building started in November 1830 at the mid-point in Kingston since improved road connections there enabled tools, men, and horses to get to the construction site. Irish immigrant laborers using pick, shovel, and wheelbarrow assisted by horse or mule-pulled scoops, dug out dirt and rock for a meager salary. An outbreak of Asiatic cholera in 1832 broke out among the workers near Princeton and spread. Dr. John Reeve of Rocky Hill treated victims with calomel, using large dosages of the mercurous chloride purgative—a common cure in early medical practice. Calomel is, however, an ineffective cure for cholera. Plain unmarked gravestones (page 116) in the Griggstown Cemetery are a reminder of those who suffered and died while the canal was under construction.

The Delaware and Raritan Canal opened to traffic in 1834. The main canal between Bordentown and New Brunswick was 44 miles long, 75 feet wide, and 8 feet deep. During the peak years between 1860 and 1880, 80 percent of the cargo in the canal was Pennsylvania coal (anthracite) for New York's industrial development. Canal traffic during this period even exceeded the Erie Canal. People who lived along the canal often put bottles up on their fences for boatmen to aim pieces of coal at. This was a way the canal residents could obtain extra coal for the winter months.

Between the Delaware, Millstone, and Raritan rivers, elevation changes were gradual and minimal. Only 14 locks were needed along the main canal. One of the earliest commercial installations of the Morse telegraph was established in Kingston and Griggstown in 1846 to monitor canal traffic, water levels, breakdowns, and speed. Other offices were at Trenton, Princeton, and New Brunswick. The canal operated 12 hours a day for about 250 days per year with toll offices on the main canal at Trenton, Princeton, Kingston, Rocky Hill, and Bound Brook. Early toll rates for "rough freight" such as sand, lime, timber, iron ore, pig iron, copper ore, and coal was 2¢ per mile. "Superior freight" such as produce, grain, and manufactured goods cost about 5¢ per ton per mile. The water level was lowered in the winter. The canal froze. In 1853, the depth of the feeder canal was increased to 8 feet and stone riprapping was installed on the main canal to prevent bank erosion. At this time, the locks were lengthened from 110 feet to 220 feet and the width remained at 24 feet.

Ratters were hired to trap muskrats that damaged the sides of the canal. He could keep the pelt and redeem noses and tails for 15¢ each. Path Walkers covered about 14 miles a day filling muskrat holes and clearing brush.

It took about two days to travel from Bordentown to New Brunswick via the canal. Before the advent of steam-driven boats in the 1850s, mule teams pulled the barges on the towpath. Wild mules were brought in from Montana and muleskinners earned $5 to $10 to train a mule for canal duty. Boat captains had to supply their own mule drivers and mules. A pair could be rented for $6 a trip. Mules usually lasted about 20 years working on the canal. Mule stables were at Bordentown, Trenton, Kingston, Griggstown, Ten Mile Run, and New Brunswick. The last vessels on the canal in the 1920s were gentlemen's yachts because of the convenient inland link between Long Island Sound and the Chesapeake Bay.

The Rocky Hill Railroad & Transportation Company constructed a spur of the Camden & Amboy Railroad that ran 2.93 miles from Kingston to the Atlantic Terra Cotta Company between Rocky Hill and Griggstown in 1864. It was thought that the canal would carry heavy and bulky freight while the railroad would handle passengers and light freight traffic. From this time on, canal business showed a steady decline as railroads began to crisscross the state. The last run of the spur to Rocky Hill was in 1928, but the line ran to the quarry until the mid-20th century. Transportation changes resulted in the end of canal operations by the close of 1932. Architects and engineers with the WPA Historic America Building Survey created drawings and photographs of certain buildings, locks, and bridges along the D&R Canal. In 1973, the Delaware and Raritan Canal and 17 structures relating to the canal were put on the National Register of Historic Places, and in 1974, the Delaware and Raritan State Park was created.

Irish immigrant laborers were employed at $1 a day between 1830 and 1834 to dig out the 44-mile main Delaware and Raritan Canal that spanned the "waist" of New Jersey. This photograph was probably taken when Carnegie Lake in Princeton was created in 1906. These hard-working men lived in tents with poor food and sanitation, often working to pay off their steerage and provision fees. Their lasting legacy is a canal that has survived for over 150 years. (Courtesy of the Delaware and Raritan Canal Commission.)

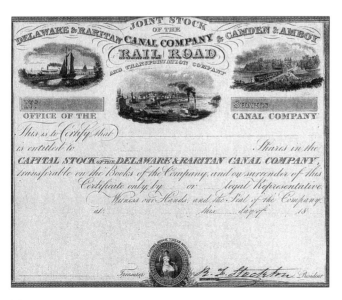

The Camden & Amboy Railroad Company and the Delaware and Raritan Canal Company both issued stocks. To the right is a stock certificate for canal stock. Robert Field Stockton's father-in-law advanced him a large sum of money to buy 4,800 shares of the canal company in 1830, which helped save its financial viability. In 1831, legislation was passed to join the two companies to guarantee completion of both the canal and the railroad. (Courtesy of the Delaware and Raritan Canal Commission.)

This photograph of the lock tender's house and telegraph-toll house on the towpath side of the Delaware and Raritan Canal in Kingston dates from 1908. The house was first occupied in 1835 by George Allen and his family. The telegraph was installed on the canal in 1846 and is believed to be one of the earliest commercial uses of telegraphic communication. The building is open to the public and occupied by the Kingston Historical Society and a Delaware and Raritan Canal State Park Ranger Office. (Courtesy of the Delaware and Raritan Canal Commission.)

This view taken from the drop gate end of lock number 8 at Kingston also shows the miter gate in the closed position. Miter gates are at the downstream end of a lock. The water flow is against closed gates at the point of the "V." The lock raises and lowers a vessel to the levels between locks. The canal elevation at Kingston is 56.3 feet and is 48.8 at lock number 9 in Griggstown. The distance between the two locks is approximately 4.5 miles. The snubbing posts on both sides of the lock were used by boatmen to secure their vessel while in the lock. (Courtesy of the Delaware and Raritan Canal Commission.)

Kingston's "A-frame" swing bridge number 16 is shown in the background of this photograph with the tender sitting on the balance beam of the lock. Eighteen vertical rods controlled the wickets within the miter gates, and the gates were opened and closed by the two wooden beams. Only one tender was needed in Kingston because the lock and the bridge were near each other. (Courtesy of the Delaware and Raritan Canal Commission.)

Behind the lock tender's house in Kingston was a mule stable for boatmen to rent fresh mules. Kingston was the mid-point on the canal and the first lock after Trenton. This stable has not been preserved and is no longer there. (Courtesy of the Historical Society of Princeton.)

Kingston's railroad station stood on the berm bank of the Delaware and Raritan Canal and was for a time a terminus for a single-track spur to Monmouth Junction, the main line. The Camden & Amboy Railroad owned the line to Kingston until 1867, when it merged with the New Jersey Railroad to become the United Jersey Railways and Canal Company. This company then merged with the Pennsylvania Railroad in 1871—the peak year of canal traffic. (Courtesy of the Kingston Historical Society.)

The boat turning basin in Kingston is between the Delaware and Raritan Canal and the railroad tracks on the east side of the canal. Vessels could pull out of the canal traffic into the basin to load and unload, make repairs, or to stay overnight. The lock tender's house can be seen in the middle background of this photograph. (Courtesy of the Kingston Historical Society.)

D. R. Canal R. Hill

The bridge tender's house at Rocky Hill on the Delaware and Raritan Canal, with a locomotive heading south towards Kingston, shows how closely the two forms of transportation were to each other. Note swing bridge number 17 on the left. The first tender's house burned in 1925 and was replaced by the one in this photograph. Jack French was the last bridge tender/ratter in Rocky Hill in 1932 when the canal closed. The State of New Jersey ordered the deteriorating tender's house to be burned in 1964. Kingston Traprock Company has created an interpretive site on the location of the old house.

Winter photographs of the Millstone River and the Delaware and Raritan Canal in Rocky Hill are scarce. This picture documents clean up and repair of a truss bridge over the river after what appears to be a flood and ice breakup. The bridge tender's house and the quarry are visible in the background.

The Rocky Hill railroad station was located on the east side of the Millstone River across the road from the canal boat turning basin. The Rocky Hill Railroad and Transportation Company was chartered in 1864. Pictured in front of the station is ticket agent John Tilton. In the background are McClosky's tavern and the smokestack of the electric power plant that operated briefly during the 1920s and 1930s. This photograph (cover photograph) is dated 1922, when the village was still a busy commercial center. The last railroad run to Rocky Hill was in 1928.

Barney McClosky's tavern on the Delaware and Raritan Canal was a favorite watering hole for boatmen, railroad workers, and other laborers in the early 20th century. Its location next to the towpath at the Rocky Hill swing bridge and railroad station on the Georgetown-Franklin Turnpike—now Route 518—was an ideal spot. Today, this spot is a parking lot for those enjoying the canal.

Griggstown's "A-frame" bridge number 18 was not located near the Griggstown lock. This view of the bridge, the tender's house on the left, and the bridge tender's station on the right has been photographed facing east from the causeway. Notice the 1.25-foot solid iron rods that support the swing bridge. The sign above the bridge reads: "Driving or riding over this bridge at a faster gait than a walk is forbidden under penalty of fine as provided by the law." (Courtesy of the Delaware and Raritan Canal Commission.)

"A-frame" bridges were replaced by "king-post" swing bridges as pictured here at the Griggstown bridge tender's house. Note the wood bulkhead to protect the pivot point from being struck by vessels in the canal. The pivot point was moved into the canal closer to the mid-point of the bridge allowing for a simpler bridge. (Courtesy of Evelyn Peters.)

Before reaching the Griggstown lock, a mule driver on the towpath heading north would have passed the 22-mile obelisk stone marker between Rocky Hill and Griggstown, which is the halfway point on the towpath. At lock number 9 is the lock tender's house, the drop gate shed, and the lock tender's station on the berm side of the canal. From the station, the tender could observe approaching vessels. (Courtesy of Shirley Staats Stryker.)

This view of lock number 9 at Griggstown shows the drawbridge and pulley at the top for the lock tender to get back and forth across the lock when he opened and closed the miter gates. In the foreground is the yacht *Mildred*. Notice the snubbing posts on the left used to control boats while they were in the lock. Locks were 24 feet wide and 110 feet long, which limited the size of vessels traveling on the Delaware and Raritan Canal. (Courtesy of the Griggstown Historical Society.)

This is a close-up view of the drop gate shed mechanism and the lock tender's house at Griggstown. The gate was in the "up" position. Rightmire's store, wheelwright shop, and mule shed can be seen in the rear of this photograph.

Originally, this building called the "Long House" was the mill hand barracks for the second gristmill at Griggstown, which was completed in 1834. It is believed that Abraham Van Doren Jr. built the mill and the barracks. The barracks were later enlarged so that mule drivers could stay overnight in what was then called the "Towpath House." Since its renovation, the building now houses a canal museum run by the Griggstown Historical Society and a Delaware and Raritan State Park ranger office. (Courtesy of the Griggstown Historical Society.)

Commercial land transportation between Rocky Hill, Kingston, and Princeton was handled by the Smalley family of Rocky Hill. Around the turn of the century, Edward A. Smalley owned a dairy farm that is now the 1860 House (Montgomery Cultural Center). His carriages took the older children to and from school in Princeton and he regularly met trains and transported out-of-town baseball teams to and from the games.

Joseph Neil was one of the drivers for the Smalley family. When the snow was too deep, the wheels were removed and runners were attached to the carriage for getting through the drifts.

PRINCETON-ROCKY HILL STAGE TIME-TABLE

Starting Place is from Post Office	Daily Except Sundays			Sundays Only	
	A. M.	P. M	P. M.	A. M.	P. M.
Leave Princeton..................	10.00	3.20	6.15	10.00	6.15
Leave Kingston...................	10.30	3.50	6.45	10.30	6.45
Arrive Rocky Hill................	11.00	4.20	7.15	11.00	7.15
Leave Rocky Hill................	7.40	1.00	5.00	8.45	5.00
Leave Kingston..................	8.10	1.30	5.30	9.15	5.30
Arrive Princeton................	8.40	2.00	6.00	9.45	6.00

Fares between Princeton and Kingston......10c one way; 15c round trip
Fares between Kingston and Rocky Hill.....10c one way; 15c round trip
Fares between Princeton and Rocky Hill.....20c one way; 30c round trip
Children under 5 years old, free; between 5 and 12, half fare.
Trunks and Packages carried.

E. A. SMALLEY, *Propr.*

A page from the 1910 *Princeton Business Directory* shows the Princeton-Kingston-Rocky Hill stage timetable and fares. This historic transportation corridor in central New Jersey enabled travelers to move around by horseback, carriage, stagecoach, train, canal boat, and even airplane! Small entrepreneurs such as the Smalleys satisfied the land transportation needs of local residents who did not have far to travel. (Courtesy of the Historical Society of Princeton.)

Smalley's transportation service spanned the horse and buggy era right into the age of the automobile. This 1914 photograph shows Smalley posing by his bus. Note the chain mechanism for turning the back wheels. School children used to call his bus a "circus wagon." When horses were no longer used, the family changed over to operating an automobile garage and dealership on Crescent Avenue in Rocky Hill (page 55) in conjunction with bus transportation.

Four
COMMERCIAL BOOM

Model makers Fred Carroll of Griggstown and Percy Ward of Rocky Hill stand in front of ornamental building decorations made at the Atlantic Terra Cotta Plant No. 3 at Rocky Hill on the east side of the Millstone River and the Delaware and Raritan Canal between Rocky Hill and Griggstown. Terra cotta as ornamentation was popular from the 1870s until the 1930s, when architectural styles changed direction again. Perth Amboy and Rocky Hill were considered to be in New Jersey's "clay belt." The manufactory employed two to three hundred workers and operated nine kilns during the peak.

Prosperity For the Villages

Transportation improvements in the first half of the 19th century created many new opportunities for business development. Although the vital main road connections had been considerably improved, it was the Delaware and Raritan Canal and the railroad that drew new commercial growth to the area. The feasibility of shipping produce and manufactured products to markets in other states via the canal and the railroad ended the earlier notion of self-sufficiency in the three villages. Those who owned mills, blacksmith and wheelwright shops, shoe and boot makers, and other small shops that had primarily served the farmers and laborers in the three villages, now witnessed larger manufacturers and businesses flourishing along the canal and the railroad.

Property began to be sold in smaller parcels enabling new entrepreneurs to develop business ventures. The Industrial Revolution reached even the smallest villages, such as Rocky Hill and Kingston, and bypassed others, such as Griggstown, which has remained a rural hamlet. The Rocky Hill area was already known as a business center because of the old copper mine and the quarry (chapter 2). Speculators and investors saw new opportunities for making money. Bulk freight could be shipped by canal, and lighter freight and passengers were transported by railroad. Fulton's steamboat made its first voyage on the Hudson River in 1807 signaling changes in water transportation. Steam power freed industry from dependence on waterpower. Transportation corridors were transforming the local landscape. Rocky Hill became a center for various manufacturing endeavors. Henry McFarlane was granted a certificate of incorporation in 1854 for the New Jersey Flax Cotton Wool Company. At the Brearley and Mount mill complex at the river, there was a gristmill, a sawmill, and a woolen mill. By 1873, the textile factory had vanished from the map and a rubber company had appeared. Fragments of these two factories remain. Kingston also had a rubber factory, and a sash and blind factory in the late 19th century.

In 1892, Nelson H. Partridge, William H. Powell, and William B. Storer built a brick factory on 4 acres of land bordering on the canal between Rocky Hill and Griggstown. In 1894, terra cotta production replaced bricks, and Powell changed the name to the Excelsior Terra Cotta Company. By 1905, three hundred workers were employed there under the direction of superintendent Louis M. Schindler. In 1907, the Excelsior and the Atlantic Terra Cotta companies consolidated as the Atlantic Terra Cotta Company; plant no. 3 in Rocky Hill employed skilled designers, technicians, and craftsmen to supply ornamental pieces for a growing construction industry. Ornamentation and tiles for the Woolworth building in New York City—the world's tallest building between 1913 and 1930—were manufactured at the Rocky Hill plant site. During the boom years of the early 20th century, the company even maintained a "company house" for visitors! Managers Philip Buchanan and Clement Baldwin Sr. both lived in Rocky Hill. The Depression beginning in 1929 eventually closed the Rocky Hill plant. The Atlantic Terra Cotta Company, with its main facility at Perth Amboy, was at that time, the largest manufacturer of architectural terra cotta in the world!

Concurrently, the Rocky Hill Quarry Company had been expanding at the end of the 19th century due to the need of stone and gravel for road and railroad building. By 1909, the renamed Delaware River Quarry Company also employed three hundred people who were mostly Italian immigrants. The quarry slowed down during the Depression, but was purchased by Linus R. Gilbert in 1933 and reopened as the Kingston Traprock quarry, which still operates today as Traprock Industries Inc. of Kingston.

Mills on the Millstone River continued to operate into the early 20th century. Both Rocky

Hill and Kingston had large mill complexes. Flour-producing gristmills, cider mills, sawmills, a plaster mill, and textile mills flourished along this part of the river. Products from these mills such as flour, grain, feed, lumber, and cloth could now be shipped by canal or by rail. Lime for the farmers was also shipped to storage buildings near the boat basins. Rocky Hill had the first gristmill in the area sometime before 1717, and Kingston's first mill was also built before 1748. Griggstown's gristmill was built by Benjamin Griggs prior to 1733. Abraham Van Doren owned the mill in Griggstown at the time it had to be torn down in 1831 for canal construction. A second mill was built on the canal but no longer exists. At various times, Griggstown also had a sawmill, a cider mill, and a stamping mill for separating the copper ore. A part of the gristmill at Rocky Hill was converted into an electric power plant in the 1930s and later was an engineering laboratory for testing materials' fatigue. While Griggstown and Rocky Hill have scant reminders of the mill era, the gristmill in Kingston, which was rebuilt after a fire in 1888, still stands and is listed on the National Historic Register. This mill continued operation until well into the 20th century.

Besides mills and manufacturers, other smaller businesses thrived throughout the one hundred-year commercial boom period. Kingston's location, midway between the two large market centers of Philadelphia and New York connected by roadways, waterways, and railways, was ideal for inns and taverns. Since Colonial times, the village had been a stopover for travellers, drivers and drovers, boatman and tenders, peddlers and preachers, and laborers of all kinds. Wealthy businessmen played a role in Kingston's business history by operating inns and transportation companies. Van Tilburgh's inn, "The Sign of the Mermaid," began operating before the Revolution and was said to be a "favorite stopping place of Washington and the governors of New Jersey." The "Beehive Inn" was also open during the Colonial period. Phineas Withington moved to Kingston and in 1811 opened an inn opposite the Sign of the Mermaid. Withington's inn and Van Tilburgh's tavern were popular stagecoach stops at the intersection of the King's Highway and what is now Laurel Street. It has been said that at times, as many as 49 stages and four hundred horses could be seen there! Other inns disappeared, such as the Beehive, the Stage Coach Inn, and the Old Heath Tavern in Kingston, Corle's tavern in Rocky Hill, and the Black Horse and Red Horse in Griggstown. At the turn of the century and into the 20th century, Barney McClosky's tavern on the canal in Rocky Hill was a popular place to wet your whistle, and the Rocky Hill Inn became a favorite summer retreat for folks from the larger cities.

The advent of the automobile, electricity, and the telephone in the early 20th century opened the way for garages and other small businesses with services and supplies more easily accessible to customers. Airplanes were designed in Rocky Hill and flown at Bolmer's Field. Richard and Elizabeth Neuhaus and their two sons arrived from Germany in 1908 and changed their name to Newhouse. Richard designed aircraft at his house on Montgomery Avenue during his spare time while he worked as a draftsman at the terra cotta plant. They moved to Washington Street where they could use the old blacksmith shop as a garage. By 1927, son Werner was helping out and the Newhouse Flying Service was up and running at what is now Princeton Airport. After the Depression in the 1930s, commercial growth slowed and the "village character" of the towns resumed.

BREARLEY & MOUNT'S MILLS.
ROCKY HILL.

An 1850 Somerset County map shows Brearley and Mount's mills in Rocky Hill. By that time, the village of Rocky Hill was developing on the west side of the Millstone River in what was then Montgomery Township. Daniel H. Mount bought a piece of property from Samuel and Maria Brearley and built a new gristmill. By 1860, son David H. Mount had added a sawmill, a plaster mill, and a woolen mill.

By 1919, the mill complex in Rocky Hill was nearly gone except for these two buildings. An electric power plant operated in the right-hand building. It was sold to Public Service Electric and Gas Co. in the 1930s. The building on the left was John N. Kenyon's Fatigue of Materials Laboratory from 1948 until 1962. All that remains today is the structure on the left, which has been altered to accommodate a business.

Rocky Hillians used to call this row of small houses "Petticoat Row" because families with many children lived here. The fathers were usually workers in the quarry or at the terra cotta factory during the 1920s. This photograph taken in 1922 on Washington Street facing east also shows the bridge over the river and the canal and the electric power plant chimney on the left.

The Stryker family operated a sawmill and lumberyard on the boat basin of the Delaware and Raritan Canal at Rocky Hill during the peak canal years. Theodore F. Stryker was the mayor of Rocky Hill from 1890 to 1891—when the village separated from Montgomery Township and became an independent borough. At that time, he lived at 169 Washington Street close to his business.

These ruins on River Road behind Trinity Episcopal Church near Van Horne Brook were the remains of a short-lived rubber factory in Rocky Hill. An 1873 *Atlas of Somerset County* shows three rubber-works buildings and the largest was on this site. It is believed that A.L. Green was the manager-owner. This photograph was made in 1922 after the factory burned. Earlier, the New Jersey Flax Cotton Wool factory was on or near this site. (Courtesy of the Historical Society of Princeton.)

For a brief time in the 1920s and 1930s, the old Hart-Polhemus mill was an electric power plant. Waterpower was used at first and later coal was burned to produce steam to operate the generators. Coal was cheap at that time. A smokestack was added and a new "Kaplan" turbine, which looked like an airplane propeller, was installed.

In 1897, when this photograph was taken, the Excelsior Terra Cotta factory operated in this strategic location on more than 100 acres next to the Delaware and Raritan Canal and the railroad. Note the floating barrel footbridge across the canal (far left), which was used for workers to get to Rocky Hill.

By 1907, the factory was called the Atlantic Terra Cotta Company. Pictured here in the main office, from left to right, are as follows: Nellie Metlar, superintendent Philip Buchanan, "Ink" Nelson, Fred Harris, George Mason, and Myrtle Van Dyke. Rocky Hill resident Reba Tilton Parsons later worked here for many years as a payroll clerk.

This piece was produced by the terra cotta plant for the front of the new Rocky Hill Hook and Ladder Company fire department building, which was dedicated in 1926. It is a blue-based plaque on white. Other terra cotta pieces may be found nearby in Griggstown, in Princeton, and on the old remaining terra cotta red brick factory powerhouse building along the canal. (Courtesy of Clem Fiori.)

After WW 1, plant no. 3 purchased more land with canal frontage, including a large company house known locally as the "Terra Cotta Hotel." This was also the terminus for the railroad spur that ran along the Delaware and Raritan Canal to Kingston and continued on to Monmouth Junction where it met the main line. (Courtesy of the Historical Society of Princeton.)

After the terra cotta pieces came out of the kilns and were cooled, joints were squared and fitted, inspected, and the finished products were marked, packed with hay, and crated for shipment. These workers appear to be posing for the camera in this early 20th-century photograph. (Courtesy of the Historical Society of Princeton.)

These shippers at the Atlantic Terra Cotta factory are helping with crating and loading decorative pieces. The process from drawing board to destination was advertised as taking no more than eight weeks. Breakage during shipment from plant no. 3 in Rocky Hill was minimal due to the seven pounds of hay used per ton of terra cotta.

Since about 1850, when Isaac Stout operated a tavern here, there has always been an inn or a tavern on the corner of Washington Street and Princeton Avenue in Rocky Hill. In 1860, Westley Morris was the proprietor of the Dey Hotel, and by 1873, the inn was called the Danley Hotel. Around 1880 (the date of this photograph), the hotel was known as Hotel Rocky Hill or the County Hotel. (Courtesy of the Historical Society of Princeton.)

William Gabriel added a third floor and the Queen Anne treatments sometime after 1881. By that time, Rocky Hill had become a fashionable, summer excursion stop-off for city folks. In the 1920s, John Toth ran the inn and a butcher shop (seen left). The Rocky Hill Inn looks much the same today except for some window changes, porch alterations, and first-floor exterior materials. Since 1945, the inn has not been a hotel but continues operation as a restaurant.

The Williamson & Griggs store at 182 Washington Street in Rocky Hill was close to the river and the canal at one of the intersections of Crescent Avenue and Washington Street. In 1850, Thomas J. Skillman's grain feed store operated here until Isaac Williamson became a partner in the 1870s and the store expanded its merchandise. The Williamsons lived at 158 Washington on what was Skillman's farm. By 1881, John Van Zandt Griggs, Williamson's son-in-law, was the new partner after Skillman's death. This close-up photograph of the store shows a sampling of wares being sold at the turn of the century. A men's Cracker Barrel Club also gathered at the store. Sammy and Minnie Cohen ran the store in the 1930s and they lived in the old post office (page 68).

The Albert T. Lewis store at 125–127 Washington Street in Rocky Hill can still be remembered by many residents because it operated until 1961, the year fire damaged it. Albert's brother, I. Morgan Lewis, added a post office next to the store after Pres. Woodrow Wilson appointed him postmaster in 1914. The store building is still there but with many alterations in appearance.

Peter and Anna (Murphy) Cortelyou managed the A&P grocery store in Rocky Hill during the early part of the century. Peter worked for the Williamson & Griggs store until he opened his own A&P in the 1920s. Madelaine and Clarence Olson ran the store in the 1930s. (Courtesy of the Historical Society of Princeton.)

The Farm and Business Directory of Hunterdon and Somerset Counties for 1914 lists three Italian men as grocers in Rocky Hill: Joseph Biomonte, John Demarco, and Charles Scasserra. Also listed is Angelo DeAngelo who operated a general store. Pictured here is John Demarco's grocery store. The Scasserra family still lives in town.

In 1924, E.A. Smalley's Rocky Hill Garage sold automobile tires for $9 and spark plugs for $1.50. Later, his son, Sydney Smalley, and his son-in-law, "Buck" Lemore, ran the garage and dealership on Crescent Avenue next to the old firehouse. Note the firehouse gong on the left.

Harold Dey's blacksmith shop in Rocky Hill appears on an 1860 map. This photograph dates from 1906. The shop was located next to a new business that was built in 1975 on this property at 133 Washington Street. Alterations to the blacksmith shop by the new owners created local concern about the historic preservation of older structures, which led to the establishment of the "historic district."

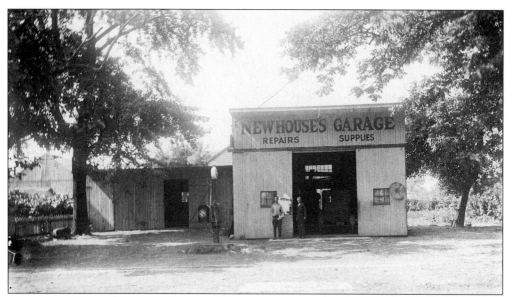

As early as 1911, Richard A. Newhouse designed and built airplanes in his garage. In the doorway of the Newhouse Garage in Rocky Hill stand two "grease monkeys" who may be Joe Neil and Raymond Cortelyou. This garage was on the same property as Dey's blacksmith shop. Planes were tested on the runway, which at that time was between Princeton Avenue and Route 206. In the 1950s, Richard E. Young, an engineer and pilot who lived on Crescent Avenue, flew people in his Chesna 210 from that runway. The runway has been relocated and is now Princeton Airport.

Pictured here is Richard A. Newhouse in an airplane that he designed. In 1929, he established the Newhouse Flying Service at Bolmar's Field, which is now Princeton Airport. People paid $1 for an airplane flight. He also gave flying instructions and put on air shows. Even during the Depression, as many as 19 aircraft were at the airport. Airmail flights took off from Princeton Airport by 1937. Richard Newhouse gave up the airport around 1942 shortly before he died. (Courtesy of the Historical Society of Princeton.)

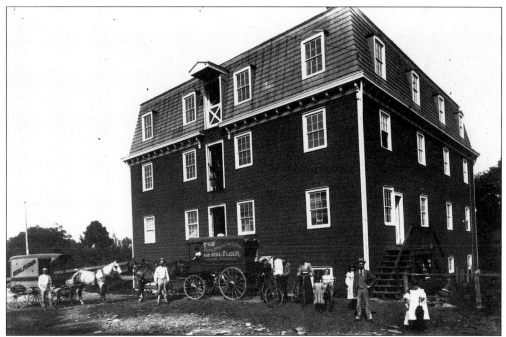

In 1797, Major John Gulick bought the Greenland-Brinston-Skillman property in Kingston (page 16) and lived there until 1828. A grandson, William Gulick, renovated the mill in a partnership with Martin Vanderveer. In 1870, the mill was sold to Charles B. Robison, who installed modern machinery (1885) and enlarged the mill. In February 1888, the mill burned. Nelson Thompson rebuilt the gristmill and operated it well into the mid-20th century. It is now part of the Kingston Mill Historic District in Princeton Township. (Courtesy of the Delaware and Raritan Canal Commission.)

This view of the Tannhauser Hotel about 1901 shows its former name, the Hoffman House. Located close to the Delaware and Raritan Canal and railroad in Kingston, this must have been a busy place for travellers and laborers. The place burned in 1910. Later, the Tannhauser became the Kingston Hotel and Rathskeller after considerable building alterations. The site is now part of the Delaware and Raritan State Park. (Courtesy of George Rightmire.)

This may have been the Old Heath Tavern at the corner of Church Street and Main Street—now Route 27 in Kingston. It is believed that this was a place to stay for people who had no money. It is still unclear whether this was the site of the earlier colonial Beehive Inn and later the Stage Coach Inn. Today, a new building on this site houses the Kingston Post Office. (Courtesy of the Kingston Historical Society.)

The Withington Inn was on this corner of the King's Highway and Heathcote Road during most of the 19th century. Phineas Withington came to Kingston in 1810 and opened this inn by 1811. Withington and Commodore Vanderbilt operated the Union Stage Line that connected the boat lines at Trenton and New York City. The Withington Inn burned in 1879 and was rebuilt as the Union Line Hotel. The building is no longer a hotel. (Courtesy of the Historical Society of Princeton.)

J.S. Woolfe's leather shoe and boot shop on Main Street in Kingston was built between 1850 and 1876. It was next to the old post office. (Courtesy of Lou Sincak.)

Luther Anthony's store in Kingston is listed in the 1914 *Hunterdon and Somerset County Farm and Business Directory*. A later owner of this store was B.S. Peebles (page 127). The building located on the corner of Route 27 and Laurel Avenue is a store and restaurant today. (Courtesy of Lou Sincak.)

The Union Garage in Kingston was one of two garages built in the 20th century to handle the increasing vehicular traffic. The other garage called the Kingston Garage was built in 1910 and has been in the Stewart family for three generations. The gentleman in the photograph proudly shows off his baby. (Courtesy of Rick Goeke.)

Petrillo's Tea Garden, or the Garden Inn, was a popular restaurant in the 1930s and 1940s. The Van Tilburg Tavern, which was built in 1754 on or near this site, was called the Sign of the Mermaid. That building was demolished in 1880. Other taverns in this area were the Millstone Inn and before that Brook's Tavern. Today, Petrillo's Tea Garden has become part of a large restaurant that includes the building on the left. (Courtesy of Rick Goeke.)

Kunze's store at the Griggstown causeway and Canal Road opened in 1927, when the Norwegian-Americans were building their summer bungalows. Michael McLean of New York City had built four bungalows here and Herman F. Kunze and his wife, Jennie Mae, converted one of these bungalows into a store. He was the owner for only four years. (Courtesy of Lloyd Van Doren.)

The Bervens bought the Kunze store in 1930. Sigurd and Alice Berven moved from Brooklyn to "Norseville" in Griggstown in 1929. Mrs. Berven had the first gas stove in town in 1930, and a pay telephone was installed in 1934. The Bervens sold the store in 1941. (Courtesy of George Rightmire.)

Edward and Rose Tornquist took over the Berven store in 1942 and they stocked many Scandinavian specialties. For 30 years, the store was a popular gathering place in Griggstown. Campers and picnickers on the meadow stopped in for penny candy or 5¢-ice cream cones. The disastrous flood of 1971 caused considerable damage to the store, and in 1972 it was sold. The building has been converted to apartments. (Courtesy of Richard Tornquist.)

The other store in Griggstown was Boices, which had been operating since the early 20th century. This photograph taken in 1910 shows the store and post office with Henry Boice in the meat wagon on the scale. Charles Cheston Sr. was the storekeeper and is weighing the wagon in this image. Boice had a telephone in the store by 1905 that improved his door-to-door butcher business. A store on this site dates back to before 1850 when E.G. Beekman owned a store. After 1854, the Oppies owned a store and post office until around 1905. The store burned in the early 1920s. (Courtesy of Lloyd Van Doren.)

This is the second gristmill in Griggstown on the Delaware and Raritan Canal swing bridge. This was built to replace the original mill that was sold when the canal was dug. This photograph probably dates from around 1900. Charles Hoagland was the last owner when the mill was demolished in 1909 and the wood was sold for building a barn elsewhere. (Courtesy of the Griggstown Historical Society.)

Frank Rocknak Sr. had a blacksmith shop at the former Honeyman house until around 1900. He then moved the shop farther south on Canal Road to the Skodacek farm. Farmers depended on wheelwrights and blacksmiths for tools, shodding horses, and wagon repairs. Paul and Rose Skodacek raised Holstein cows, and every morning and evening their cows would be herded across the canal bridge to the meadow between the canal and the river. (Courtesy of the Griggstown Historical Society.)

A photograph of Rocky Hill at the Millstone River in the 1920s shows the village with several buildings clustered around the major commercial area. The electric power plant is on the right. Little is left of these structures today. This area is a floodplain.

This view of Kingston taken in 1906 is a composite of many of the business activities that flourished as a result of the canal and railroad. Fisk's grocery store is on the left, the lock tender's house and gristmill is in the center rear, and the Tannhauser Hotel is on the right. (Courtesy of Rick Goeke.)

Five

SERVING PEOPLE'S
OTHER NEEDS

Between 1901 and 1928, George A. Woolfe was the postmaster in Kingston. At that time, the post office was near the corner of Laurel Avenue and Main Street (Route 27) in Kingston next to Woolfe's shoe shop. He ran a confectionery and ice cream shop there as well. Earlier in 1881, another post office was run from Cornelius Van Duyne's store. The present post office is at the corner of Church Street and Route 27. (Courtesy of Rick Goeke.)

Communication and Protection

Rocky Hill is the only one of the three villages that is an independent borough operating within Somerset County. Ever since 1890, the borough has elected its own mayor, borough council, and school board. Kingston's historic areas are located in three different counties: Mercer, Middlesex, and Somerset. Municipal administration of Kingston today is managed by the townships of Franklin in Somerset County and South Brunswick in Middlesex County. Griggstown's historical areas today reach into the townships of Franklin and Montgomery in Somerset County, but the center of the hamlet is in Franklin Township. None of the three villages has a local police force. Rocky Hill has a constable. The villages are dependent upon township or state police for the enforcement of law and order.

During early Colonial times, mail was delivered to only three towns in the Province: Perth Amboy, Trenton, and Burlington. By 1754, service improved and mail was delivered on horseback to a local inn or tavern where people could pick it up. Part of getting the mail was hearing the latest news. Gradually, post offices were set up in a local store and eventually, local postmasters were appointed according to the political party in power. The rural free delivery system of direct-to-the-home delivery was initiated in 1896 and was championed by farmers and mail order houses like Sears Roebuck and Montgomery Ward, but opposed by local storekeepers. Today, residents in Kingston and Rocky Hill's historic districts have boxes at the local post office, and Griggstown residents and those outside of the center of Kingston and Rocky Hill have rural mail delivery.

In Rocky Hill, the location of the post office was at the whim of the postmaster. Theodore Stryker, for example, built a new building in 1897 for the post office across from the Williamson & Griggs store. Things did change and by 1914, I. Morgan Lewis was appointed postmaster by Pres. Woodrow Wilson. Mr. Lewis built a room onto his general store to receive and distribute the mail.

The post office in Griggstown was located in the Mule Tender's Barracks (page 40) for over 25 years until around 1905 when Harvey Boice bought the former Oppie store across the canal causeway. Each family had a pigeonhole behind the counter and a postal clerk handed out the mail. Later, locked boxes were installed. At that time, mail was delivered from Princeton to all the families living around Griggstown. The Boice store (page 62) burned in 1920 and the post office moved temporarily to the home of Charles Cheston (page 90) until rural free delivery began. The Princeton Post Office still delivers mail to Griggstown residents on the east side of the Millstone River. There is no post office in Griggstown.

Kingston had the advantage of being on the colonial Old Post Road and probably received mail more quickly than Griggstown and Rocky Hill throughout the 18th and 19th centuries. Just as in the other villages, the post offices were most often found in grocery stores in the 20th century until federal post office buildings were constructed. Both Kingston and Rocky Hill have post offices now.

Rocky Hill's first firehouse was behind the old borough hall on the corner of Princeton Avenue and Crescent Avenue. The Rocky Hill Hook and Ladder Company No. 1 was organized in 1902 and soon after in 1905, a hand-drawn pumper was purchased. A Ladies Auxiliary was also active in fund-raisers as well as social functions. A new firehouse was completed by 1926 and a tradition of carnivals was started, which continued until the last one in 1960. The volunteer First Aid and Rescue Squad was formed in 1949 and the members themselves constructed a building for housing an ambulance.

The Kingston Volunteer Fire Company No. 1 was founded in 1924 after the Kingston

Improvement Association had put out a rapidly spreading fire. The department serves both Franklin and South Brunswick townships in the Kingston area. Their first building was a former mortuary garage and their present firehouse is on Heathcote Brook Road. The Kingston First Aid Squad was incorporated in 1972 as an independent organization but works closely with the fire department.

The Griggstown Volunteer Fire Company was founded in 1946 after the Griggstown Improvement Association determined that the hamlet had enough homes to warrant a fire company. Rocky Hill had been one of the companies to service Griggstown prior to that time. By 1952, a firehouse was completed next to the cemetery on Canal Road. A Women's Auxiliary assists with fund-raising and social events.

Small towns without their own police force sought other means of maintaining law and order. Various "protective associations" were formed by citizens to guard against vagrants, peddlers, and homeless people. After the Civil War, there were major population shifts and new waves of immigration, as labor was sought for industrial development and transportation expansion. A fear of being overwhelmed by this uprootedness and growing disorder seemed a threat to small pastoral communities. A solid middle class, protective of commercial development, had also developed and suburbia was born.

The forerunner of police departments were volunteer "Vigilante Societies." In the beginning, during the early 19th century, their main concern was horse thefts. After the automobile arrived, these organizations helped with other policing. The Griggstown Pursuing and Detection Society was incorporated in 1881 and was a part of countywide policing efforts. Seventeen "pursuers" were appointed to cover specific areas. In 1900 William Oppie, a grocer, was assigned to monitor Griggstown. Pursuers even wore badges and were permitted to make arrests for disorderly conduct. Kingston also had a "Protective Association" whose members included prominent citizens of the community.

Rocky Hill had a somewhat different approach because after 1890, the borough hired a marshal and later a constable to carry out local ordinances. The 1915 Borough Ordinances outlines that marshals "shall have the power to arrest upon view, without warrant, and bring before the borough recorder or mayor . . . any person whom they may see committing a breach of the peace or violating any law of the State or ordinance of the borough." In 1915, Rocky Hill had an ordinance establishing a "police department," which was actually the "police committee" of the Borough Council and the marshal. An ordinance was passed that same year "relating to the morals, peace and good order of the Borough of Rocky Hill." Several other ordinances were similarly passed to control disruptive behavior. Rocky Hill also had a small jail next to the old fire department.

The State of New Jersey is currently assessing and redefining municipalities in order to design planning objectives for the state. Rocky Hill and Kingston qualify as "villages." This means that they are less than a square mile in area, have a population of more than 250 people, have more than 75 housing units, and employ more than 50 people. Griggstown, on the other hand, is classed as a "hamlet," which is the smallest unit of "municipal center designation." The population of all three historic village centers has stabilized with little or no room for further large-scale development.

The residence today at 165 Washington Street in Rocky Hill was once a post office. It was built in 1897 by Theodore Stryker with the intention of converting the building to a home after his term as postmaster was up. He succeeded A.T. Lewis as postmaster. In the 1930s, Sammy and Minnie Cohen lived in the house, and later Carmen Panicaro lived there.

The permanent location for the Rocky Hill Post Office is at 130 Washington Street in the center of town. This photograph dates from the 1960s before the building was changed and enlarged. Jim O'Malley was the postmaster at the time. Earlier, William H. Buchanan ran a barbershop here with a few pool tables and a nickelodeon. He also sold cigars and tobacco.

After Rocky Hill became an independent borough in 1890, Voorhees Hall became the headquarters for the newly-established municipal government offices and an adjacent jail. The land had been donated by the widow of Abraham O. Voorhees, Abigail Vanderveer Voorhees. After the former Van Horne tract had been divided up, the Vanderveer family had bought 95 acres on Princeton Avenue.

For more than one hundred years, the small village of Rocky Hill has functioned with its own government. The 60-page borough operating procedures and ordinances of 1915 provide a glimpse into the history of small-town government in New Jersey. (Courtesy of Raymond E. Whitlock Jr.)

4   BOROUGH OF ROCKY HILL

BOROUGH OFFICERS 1915

Mayor
PHILIP D. BUCHANAN

Members of Council
EDWIN S. VOORHEES, President
RALPH W. AVERY
WALTER E. BEERS
I. MORGAN LEWIS
HOWARD S. VOLK
GEO. H. DONOVAN

Borough Clerk...................C. R. Baldwin
Asessor.....................George W. Mason
Collector.......................Malvern Reeve
Chosen Freeholder..............Louis E. Opie
Recorder.................Frederick W. Harris
Chairman of Street Committee...E. S. Voorhees
Chairman of Police and Fire Com...W. E. Beers
Chairman of Finance and Auditing Com.....
                      Geo. H. Donovan
Overseer of Poor................J. V. Z. Griggs

Board of Health
Wm. N. Stults, President
C. R. Baldwin
Secretary and Registrar of Vital Statistics
M. Reeve, M. D., Physician

The Rocky Hill Hook and Ladder Company No. 1 poses in front of the old firehouse behind Voorhees Hall on Crescent Avenue. The firehouse burned in the 1960s.

After the fire company was founded in 1902, a chemical cart called the "Rex" was bought in 1905 and became the department's logo. This historic piece of equipment is still owned by the company and is paraded on significant holidays. (Courtesy of the Rocky Hill Hook and Ladder Company.)

The new firehouse was dedicated in 1926 with partial funding from the Atlantic Terra Cotta Company. Members of the Rocky Hill Hook and Ladder Company pose for this 1948 photograph. The members, from left to right, are as follows: (front row) Percy Ward, Clair Marsh, Garrett Durling, Carlo Perantoni, George Mason, Raymond Breese, Malvern Reeve, Martin Breese, Raymond Durling, Nicholas Diaforli, Clarence Schlapfer, Rankin Wright, Raymond E. Whitlock, Raymond C. Whitlock, Harry Stryker, Harry Thompson, Louis Robotti, Bernard McClosky, and Dan Hoffman; (back row) George Fields, Steve Bognar, Gilbert Ireland, Clarence Lovey, Wilbur Lowe, Otto Young, Edward Buchanan, Edward McVaugh, Art Case, and Howard Speinheimer. (Courtesy of the Rocky Hill Hook and Ladder Company.)

The Rocky Hill First Aid and Rescue Squad was organized in 1949 with Steve Bognar as president. In 1952, members constructed a building to garage rescue equipment. This volunteer group purchased this 1962 Cadillac ambulance for $12,000 in cash.

Charter members of the Griggstown Volunteer Fire Company bid farewell to Herb Friedberg, who was president in 1946. Pictured from left to right are as follows: Charles Battle, Hunt Corrigen, Fred Carroll, Ken Green, John Wallek, John Langfeldt, John Rightmire, David Klieber, Andrew Marck, Edward Tornquist, David Smith, Arthur Carroll, Lloyd Van Doren, Thor Rosfjord, Leroy Strasburger, Karl Holst, Arthur Sandvik, Stanley Madsen, John Langfeldt Sr., Paul Skodacek, Herb Freeberg, Micky Madsen, Eiven Hilsen, Oswald Hoepfner, Steve Galick, Ray Peters, and Ernest Camp. This photograph was made by George Rightmire, the first president of the fire company, at the Friedberg house (old Beekman House). (Courtesy of the Griggstown Volunteer Fire Company.)

Fund-raisers for the Griggstown Volunteer Fire Co. began as soon as it was founded in 1946. The Griggstown Improvement Association had recommended the establishment of a local fire department. The meadows in town were a perfect place for a clambake fund-raiser. Pictured from left to right are as follows: Ray Peters, Stanley Madsen, Arthur Carroll, and John Marck. (Courtesy of the Griggstown Volunteer Fire Company.)

Two early fire trucks are parked at Ed and Rose Tornquist's store in the center of Griggstown in the 1940s. Ed Tornquist was the first fire chief. The engine on the left was bought from Pennington and was called the "gray ghost" because it was painted gray. The "Reo" on the right was an American LaFrance on a Brockway chassis and came from Kingston. (Courtesy of the Griggstown Volunteer Fire Company.)

The Griggstown Volunteer Fire Company had raised sufficient money to complete a firehouse on Canal Road by 1949. It is located next to the Griggstown Cemetery. (Courtesy of the Griggstown Volunteer Fire Company.)

Kingston Volunteer Fire Department No. 1 was organized in 1924. A building near the Presbyterian church caught fire and spread rapidly to other structures. Citizens then wanted their own fire company. J. Watson Shann was a charter member of the fire company and in 1926, his widow sold his old mortuary hearse garage on Railroad Avenue (now Heathcote Road) to the fire department for their first building. The first fire truck was delivered by railroad. (Courtesy of Rick Goeke.)

A new firehouse was built in the 1930s on Heathcote Road in South Brunswick on the same property. Up until 1926, Heathcote Road was called Railroad Avenue. In the 1950s, an addition was put on the firehouse for the new 1958 Ward La France truck. (Courtesy of Rick Goeke.)

Members of the Kingston Volunteer Fire Company No. 1 in the 1940s are pictured from left to right as follows: (front row) Chester Potts, George Kaltschmid Jr., Jack Luck, Armand Petrillo (president), George Kaltschmid Sr., William Bursher, Robert Brian, and Dave Taglioli; (back row) John Casnaly, Joe Catelli, George Kirby, Rocky Devito, William Kuderka, Les Luck, Ralph Klieber, Raymond Wolfe, and Harry Place. (Courtesy of George Luck Jr.)

This 1939 Dodge crash truck with special lights for night automobile rescues became an important 20th-century means of coping with the increasing traffic in the area. The fire department works closely with other area emergency service organizations.

MEMBERS OF THE
KINGSTON PROTECTIVE ASSOCIATION

OFFICERS FOR 1911

B. L. GULICK, President

D. D. SUYDAM, Vice-President

JOHN C. STRYKER, Sec'y and Treas.

DIRECTORS

Alexander Bastedo   Luther Anthony

George A. Wolf

MEMBERS

Anthony, Luther
Bastedo, Alexander
Farr, Reuben
Green, C. D.
Gulick, B. L.
Harris, James D.
Hawk, E. H.
Higgins, Martin
Higgins, Johnty
Hoffman, Daniel
Lake, Samuel H.
McFaul, John J.
Mershon, Charles E.
Merrill, Jos. A.
Mount, G. W.

Okeson, Charles
Potts, Wilbur E.
Shann, J. Watson
Smith, Clinton H.
Stonaker, George
Stryker, John C.
Stryker, S. Paxson
Stults, Harvey
Suydam, D. D.
Thompson, Nelson
Tichnor, Alonzo
Webster, J. Charles
Wolf, George A.
Wolf, William F.

This was a poster announcing Kingston's Protective Association for the year 1911. The names of many storekeepers and small businessmen of the time appear among the membership. Perhaps somewhat like today's "crime watch" neighborhoods, these men took responsibility for guarding against disorderly conduct, liquor licenses, and theft. (Courtesy of Lou Sincak.)

Six

SCHOOLS, HOMES, AND CULTURAL ACTIVITIES

Griggstown school children in 1921 are pictured here under the guidance of their teacher, Caroline Carroll. A few of the children can be identified: Dorothy and Ruth Rightmire (front row left), Charles Cheston (second row far right), and Fred Carroll (seated to the left of Charles). (Courtesy of Lloyd Van Doren.)

Making Life Meaningful

Portraits of George Washington and Abraham Lincoln hung above young school children in just about every one-room schoolhouse in the country after the Civil War. Presidential heroes represented the characteristics teachers hoped to bring out in their students. Such idealism is difficult to imagine today. William and Alexander McGuffey's Eclectic Readers were in schools between 1836 and 1922 with their emphasis on reading, elocution (speaking), and spelling. Palmer penmanship, geography, and the multiplication tables were also stressed in schools, as curriculums developed after the 1846 state legislation creating public schools. By 1871, free schools were mandated.

The Griggstown Historical Society headquarters are in the Griggstown School, an early 19th-century one-room schoolhouse that has been preserved much as it was in the 1840s when it was built. In 1854, the school was moved behind the Griggstown Reformed Church and in 1960, was moved again farther back from the church. There was only one teacher. Most of them came from Pennsylvania, where there were more teachers' training schools. Teachers were paid about $30 a month and later, $50, and they paid $8 to $10 to board with local families. Students attended until grade eight and then chose to attend high school in New Brunswick, Bound Brook, or Princeton. The school was auctioned off in 1932 and was ultimately purchased by the church for $207.

Riverside School on the western side of the Millstone River at Griggstown operated from 1812 until 1912. Griggstown residents who lived in what is now Belle Mead in Montgomery Township attended this school. A new schoolhouse was built in 1912 and was sold in 1928 after the school was consolidated with Harlingen School. The two schools competed with one another in spelling bees and ball games. M. Louise Crawford was the last teacher at both of the schools.

Rocky Hill's first public school, called the Rocky Hill School, opened in 1848 on land at the corner of Main Street (now Washington Street) and Montgomery Avenue. Isaac Stout sold the property to school trustees, John Skillman, Samuel Brearley, and Garret Schenck for $40. In 1879, it cost $501.25 to educate the students who attended! Teachers were paid $35 a month and the building seated up to one hundred youngsters. In those days, rural students attended the nearest school. This school was one of ten district grade schools in Montgomery Township until 1890, when Rocky Hill became an independent borough. For the next 18 years, the school was operated by the Borough of Rocky Hill until the new school was built.

Washington School on Montgomery Avenue opened in 1908 and offered kindergarten through grade eight until 1962, when Rocky Hill began sending elementary school students to Montgomery Township schools. High school students attended Princeton High School until 1967 when an agreement was made with the township to pay per student tuition for high school students as well. Rocky Hill Borough has its own board of education and is a "sending district" for students to attend Montgomery Township schools. Flora Silcox is perhaps remembered as the most influential teacher-principal at that school.

Kingston's oldest school was a private academy associated with the Presbyterian church on the cemetery side of Main Street (now Route 27). Before public free education, it was the obligation of churches to educate young people beyond family training. Little is known about this academy except that the Kingston Library Company was formed in 1812 and used the school as its headquarters. A school was also on the corner of Main Street and Academy Street before public schools were mandated. This building no longer stands. In 1871, the Kingston Free School was built on the opposite side of Academy Street and was operated by South

Brunswick Township Board of Education. It was not until 1920, that another school was built in Kingston on Laurel Avenue in Franklin Township. Both of these buildings remain but are no longer schools. Route 27 is the dividing line in Kingston between two townships and two counties. The village of Kingston today sends students to both township school systems.

Other private academies and schools were established in the villages. Aaron Colby ran a private school in Kingston after 1835 charging $1 to $3 per quarter. The Scudder-Collver School in Griggstown was a girls' school in the 1940s where historian Paul Marshall Allen taught. He was the son-in-law of Herbert J. Friedberg (page 72) of Buttonwood Farm—the old Beekman estate—and wrote historical articles about Griggstown.

All three of the villages are on the National Register of Historic Places, which helps the communities preserve and maintain sites and structures of historic interest. The houses in Rocky Hill, Griggstown, and Kingston reflect a variety of architectural styles. Many 18th-century houses burned and have been rebuilt in other styles. Early Dutch houses were typically small and were built of stone or wood. After the Revolution and by the turn of the century, Federal-style houses became popular. Greek Revival, gothic Revival, and Italianate styles were common until the industrialization after the Civil War, when mass-produced building materials allowed for very decorative treatments on buildings and houses. Late Victorian architecture included the Italianate style, French Second Empire houses with mansard roofs, Queen Anne, Eastlake, and exotic Victorian-gothic houses. Examples of 20th-century bungalows and the prairie style are also found in the villages.

Theater, music, dances, school programs, clubs, Chautauqua touring shows, and libraries provided a broad range of cultural experiences for people of all ages and backgrounds. Kingston even had its own newspaper called *The Kingston Record* in the 1830s. Various buildings in town were used for public events. Churches, schools, halls, and firehouses often served this purpose. Princeton and Rutgers Universities are nearby, but until the popularity of the automobile, these cultural centers were inaccessible to most people. New immigrants were urged to learn English as soon as possible. Atlantic Terra Cotta workers with diverse names and languages were given instruction to ease their assimilation. Minstrel shows in Kingston brought together African-American neighbors with the auxiliary to produce shows that raised funds for the fire department. Local bands and choral groups were composed of immigrants as well as longtime residents.

In the early 1900s, Lyric Hall in Rocky Hill became a center of many social and cultural activities. Silent movies were shown with Mildred Robbins at the organ or Reba Parsons at the piano. Live theatrical shows were staged and the room was even used for basketball games. Once a church, this building near the center of town brought folks together for entertainment before television and computer screens altered leisure time activities.

Kingston's library was one of the earliest in the area. It was a company with shareholders and officers. The original company, dating from 1812, had 70 members and owned 284 books. Names of people in Princeton, Kingston, Rocky Hill, and environs may be found on the roster. The Kingston Circulating Library was probably still in existence as late as 1886. Griggstown had the opportunity for a library when the canal closed and the bridge tender's station became a public library in 1932. It was the smallest county library until it closed in 1970.

The Rocky Hill School was the first public school in town. It was built in 1848 in the Greek Revival style and operated from 1848 until 1908 when a new school was built. One hundred students could be seated—if all attended. William S. Durling bought the property on the corner of Washington Street and Montgomery Avenue in 1914 and turned the building into a two-story house.

This is a late 19th-century class photograph of the Rocky Hill School. Miss Johnson was one of the teachers who taught the children reading, writing, and arithmetic. The entrance and cupola have now been changed.

Washington School on Montgomery Avenue in Rocky Hill was completed in 1908, and grades kindergarten to eight were taught here until 1962. Teachers there were Miss Annie Cheston, Miss Mildred Knies, Miss Lillian Buchanan, Miss Loreta Silcox, and Mrs. Raymond Cortelyou. The Flemish-bond brick building is now the Rocky Hill Borough Hall.

Mrs. Flora M. Silcox was a teacher and later a principal at the Washington School during her 35-year educational career. She taught grades six, seven, and eight upstairs. She is still remembered today by residents who attended school there. (Courtesy of A. Theodore Merritt.)

Older students are standing with their teacher around 1920 at the Washington School. A few names of students in this photograph are listed from left to right: (first row) Ray Durling, Sidney Howard, Clarence Olsen, and Charlie Howard; (second row) Irene Bowen, Alma Vreeland, Ann Mae Baldwin, and Leola Breese Butler; (back row) Mary Ross, Loreta Silcox, Katherine Van Pelt, and Rose Panicaro. Those who went on to high school after grade eight attended Princeton High School until 1967. (Courtesy of Clem Baldwin.)

June 18, 1924, was the date of this graduation photograph taken at the Washington School in Rocky Hill. This graduating class was the largest ever from Washington School. Commencement exercises were held at Lyric Hall with music furnished by Vreeland's orchestra. Some of the 13 graduates are missing in the picture. Graduating were Katherin E. Longstreet, Albert R. Lewis, Constance N. Ballassy, Donald C. Barrowman, Mary Crovette, Mary Ellen McCarthy, Ruth E. Newhouse, Elizabeth M. Reinbeck, Kathryn E. Volk, John E. Frank, Everett M. Lewis, John Panicaro, and Anthony Scasserra. (Courtesy of Peggy Harris.)

Riverside School, on the west side of the Millstone River in Griggstown, was the oldest of the two schools in town. It was built sometime prior to 1812, when Major John Baird leased the building to be used as a district school. (Courtesy of Shirley Staats Stryker.)

The old schoolhouse was replaced in 1912 by this building. It was later moved farther back on the lot and eventually became a garage. In 1928, the property was sold to William H. Graeber, who later married Anna M. Kunze, and they operated an egg wholesale business there. Griggstown's last dairy farmer, Duncan Campbell, and Lloyd Van Doren were among the students who attended Riverside. In 1927, the school was consolidated with Harlingen. (Courtesy of Shirley Staats Stryker.)

The Griggstown School was built in the 1840s. The earlier board and baton style on the exterior was later replaced. The building is now the headquarters of the Griggstown Historical Society, which was founded in 1978. (Courtesy of the Griggstown Historical Society.)

This late 19th-century photograph of younger students at the Griggstown School shows two women, it is unknown which one was the teacher. (Courtesy of the Griggstown Historical Society.)

Students at the Kingston Free School on Academy Street in South Brunswick pose during the 1930s. They are pictured from left to right as follows: (front row) Eric Zapf, Roland Teamer, Ted Catelli, Joe Catelli, and Raymond Burnett; (middle row) Matt Feldman, Earl Snedeker, Pete Van Note, Howard Snedeker, Chester Potts, Hazel Lewis, and Mildred Randolph; (back row) Margaret Kaltschmid, Grace Barlow, Bernice Teamer, Hazel Updike, Jesse Anderson, unidentified, Betty Van Note, Audrey Langer, Mr. Richards, Agnes Meyers, and Ada Burnett. (Courtesy of Rick Goeke.)

This photograph was taken on December 16, 1933 in front of the Kingston School in Franklin Township. The students in grades five through eight are pictured here. The students, from left to right, are as follows: Josephine Petrillo, Lillian Harris, Donald Yarrow, Madelyn Wilson, Gertrude Eisenberger, ? Yarrow (sister of Donald), Margaret Brabson, Katheryn Higgins, John Willett, Florence Burke, Ruth Willett, Dorothea Potts, Irene Higgins, Philip Wesp, Dorothy Higgins, Robert Herrman, Mary Lackey, Benjamin Herrman, Katherine ?, John Brabson Jr., Frank Piccasia, Raymond Higgins, Floyd Wilson Jr., Mr. Lois Kruschnitt (teacher), unidentified. This photograph was taken by Carl H. Van Nordheim of Kingston.

This large property on Washington Street in Rocky Hill was once the Vanderveer-Vreeland farm. The right half of the main house was probably added by Dr. John Reeve between 1793 and 1815. It operated as a farm until 1955. Much of it was later sold for Princeton Ridge development in the 1960s. The house and several other buildings still remain on this smaller property. (Courtesy of the Historical Society of Princeton.)

Another large farm in Rocky Hill was the Abraham Voorhees 100-acre property carved out of Van Horne land. The house was built between 1840 and 1845 and the farm operated as a dairy farm in the second half of the 19th century. The large barn complex was probably built some years after the house. The Sweeney family lived here on Princeton Avenue in the early 20th century and donated land for the St. James Catholic Church. Flowers for commercial markets were also raised here. (Courtesy of the Historical Society of Princeton.)

This gracious vernacular Greek Revival-style home at 169 Washington Street in Rocky Hill was built by Thomas J. Skillman in 1845 on the site of a much smaller 1795 house. Greek Revival homes were built during the period of 1820 until 1860. The side bay windows were probably added by Theodore Stryker, who later lived in the house. Teacher-principal Flora Silcox also lived here at one time. This photograph was taken around 1900.

The Stout-Skillman House at 98 Washington Street in Rocky Hill is a pattern-book Italianate-Tuscan Revival house built around 1845 on land then belonging to Isaac Stout and his son-in-law, Thomas J. Skillman. Italianate houses were popular between 1840 and 1880 and are almost square with wide eaves supported by large brackets. Later, the house was owned by the Vreeland family who grew flowers for commercial markets. This photograph was taken in 1920.

Theodore F. Stryker, Rocky Hill's lumber baron, built what is now called the Stryker-Gil House at 101 Washington Street. This lovely Eastlake-style Victorian home was built in the last quarter of the 19th century (1870 to 1890 period). The mechanical lathe allowed for decorative and elaborate woodwork on the exterior and interior of these houses. This photograph was taken around 1914.

This Second Empire house, with its mansard slate roof, at 10 Crescent Avenue in Rocky Hill was built before 1880. The symmetrical square block look was popular from 1860 to 1890. At one time, Dr. Malvern Reeve (page 120) lived here. The house burned in 1994 and has been completely reconstructed.

There are two pattern-book Queen Ann houses at 118 and 122 Washington Street in Rocky Hill built by Edward Stout of Kingston in 1911 and 1912. I. Morgan Lewis lived in 118 and Albert T. Lewis in 122, the one shown here. Queen Anne-style houses were very popular between 1880 and 1900 during the Victorian period. Asymmetrical, with a variety of colors and materials, these homes show creative use of glass and woodwork.

"Woodside" on River Road between Rocky Hill and Kingston was the McFarlane family home for many years. Henry McFarlane built the N.J. Flax Wool and Cotton factory and donated the land for Trinity church. This photograph was taken in 1922 after William inherited the house and 173 acres from his parents, Henry and Ann Buchanan McFarlane. The house burned and became known as the "spook house" by local children. Traprock Company of Kingston is now headquartered on the site.

This is an example of an early Dutch house built in the late 1700s in Griggstown on the Millstone River. Cornelius Simonsen lived there and the farm came to be called the "Old Simonsen Place." Built in the Dutch tradition, the thick plaster walls contain a mixture of mud, straw, hay, and animal hair. This photograph shows the house in 1900 shortly before Byron Cheston purchased it in 1912. (Courtesy of the Griggstown Historical Society.)

River Bend farm in Griggstown was originally the Christopher Hoagland farm during the Colonial period. Several succeeding generations of Hoaglands have lived here since 1727, when it was built. It is on the west side of the Millstone River in Montgomery Township across from the former old mill. The property is no longer a farm. (Courtesy of Shirley Staats Stryker.)

Veghte family members were early Dutch land buyers in Griggstown in the early 1700s. Gerrit bought land on the east side of the Millstone River and grandsons Gerrit Jans and Nicolas Jans lived there. This photograph shows one of the Veghte houses. This one is on Canal Road and was built in the Italianate style in 1888 to replace an older one that burned. (Courtesy of Evelyn Peters.)

This house on the corner of Coppermine and Canal Roads had been owned by Franz Hellriegel in the early 20th century. When the house was later owned by a New York lawyer named Sterling, he called his home "Stepping Stones" and placed Atlantic Terra Cotta unicorn heads at the entrance driveway. In the 1940s, it became a private school for young ladies called the Scudder-Collver School. By 1947, the school no longer operated in Griggstown and the house briefly became a Christian Scientist retreat. (Courtesy of Shirley Staats Stryker.)

Jedediah Higgins arrived in Kingston in 1709 as a squatter without gaining title to his land from the East Jersey Proprietors. The story is, however, that he purchased 1,000 acres from the Lenni Lenape Indians for a sow and a litter of pigs. The original house on today's Route 27 and Raymond Road is thought to have been built before 1714 and has since been enlarged and remodeled. (Courtesy of Rick Goeke.)

During the 1880s and 1890s, minstrel shows blossomed into large-scale entertainment by large touring companies. African Americans had billing in these programs and, as this photograph shows, were also a part of local shows in Kingston. The Ladies Auxiliary of the Kingston fire company put on minstrel shows in the 1930s for fund-raising. Minstrel shows are no longer considered appropriate entertainment. (Courtesy of George Luck Jr.)

The Atlantic Terra Cotta Company provided instructors for new immigrants to learn English. The men met weekly at Trinity Episcopal Church in Rocky Hill. This company photograph was taken in 1924. Pictured from left to right are as follows: (front row) "Happy Jack" Frank, Joseph Raduzycki, George Panicaro, Charles Scassera, Mike Frank, and unidentified; (middle row) Frank Amalfitano, John Cociolilo, George Message, Charles Frank, Steve Sharon, Jerry Ruggear, Charles Luchini, Joe Ruggear, and Gus Cialell; (back row) Mike Ruggear (instructor), John Joy, Charles Ruggear, Roger McNally, "Little" John (surname unknown), Jack Crovetto, Saveria Ciallella, unidentified, Reed (instructor), unidentified, and unidentified.

Once the Methodist Episcopal Church at 10 Princeton Avenue in Rocky Hill, this building became known as Lyric Hall in the early 1900s and became the center of many community functions. Albert T. Lewis, grocery storeowner and handyman, ran silent movies there and live theatrical performances. Basketball games and other community events were held here as well. This photograph is dated 1922.

"On the Little Big Horn"

PRESENTED BY

THE ROCKY HILL Y. M. C. A.

Saturday Eve'g, March 10

NEW LYRIC THEATRE

CAST OF CHARACTERS

Major Paul Ludlow, an officer of the 47th U. S. Calvary.............
Raymond Cortelyou.
Lieut. Henry Winston, A West Pointer................Alfred Merritt
William Carleton, an Indian agent......................Joseph Neil
Gen. Horace Graham, Commandant of Fort Winslow....William Volk
Dakota Dan, a scout on Federal Service...............William Reed
Patrick O'Rafferty, a troop sergeant...............William Hixson
War Eagle, a Sioux Chief.........................Garrett Durling
Hop Sing, a Chinese cook...........................Sidney Smalley
Bill Hanks, a telegraph operator ⎞
Sam Martin, a trooper ⎠ ....Dayton Buchanan
Beryl Seymour, The Belle of the Garrison...........Rose Purrington
Rose-of-the-Mist, a Sioux maiden.......................Sarah Bird
Sue Graham, niece of Gen. Graham................Lavinia Stewart
Mrs. Caroline Spencer, a widow with a fondness for Botany.........
Mrs. Walter E. Beers

Place, Montana————Time, 1875

SCENES

Act. 1—Exterior of Ft. Winslow—An abduction and oath.
Act 2—The cabin in the hills—The Indian attack.
Act 3—Room in Ft. Winslow—The reprieve.
Act 4—Same as act 1—The atonement.

SYNOPSIS:

Act 1—A doubting sergeant. News of the Indian uprising. The abduction. A soldier's oath. To the rescue. Then justice.
Act 2—Troubles of a Botanist. Hop Sing makes soup of Botanical Specimens. The Indians are coming. The story. The avowal of love. "We will fight to the end and die together." The attack. The battle. The rescue.
Act 3—A message from the president. The wire is cut. A soldier's despair. I believe you innocent. The verdict. The agent's message. Beryl to the rescue. The race after the President. The reprieve.
Act 4—A widow's lament. I love ye, Rose. Story of the Massacre. The inheritance. Hop Sing goes on strike. Carleton in Disguise returns. Rose shoots Carleton. The reunion. "It is God's way."

Director—Mrs. Flora M. Silcox.   Music—Orchestra.

This play was staged by the Rocky Hill YMCA at the Lyric Theater in 1917. Mrs. Flora M. Silcox directed the play and many names of local residents at that time may be seen in the list of "actors."

The Rocky Hill Band drew most of its members from the Atlantic Terra Cotta factory during the 1930s when this photograph was made. The conductor appears to be in the middle. The house in the rear is the Buchanan-Whitlock house at 2 Park Avenue. At one time, the superintendent of the factory lived here. (Courtesy of the Historical Society of Princeton.)

John F. Rightmire Jr. of Griggstown posed in 1910 for a formal portrait with his band uniform and coronet. He was a payroll clerk at the terra cotta factory and also played in several area bands. Today, the Blawenburg Band is the only one of these community bands still in existence. (Courtesy of George Rightmire.)

NAMES

OF THE

PRESENT PROPRIETORS

OF THE

KINGSTON LIBRARY COMPANY.

— ❊ —

1 David Comfort,
2 Erkuries Beatty,
3 Mary W. Ferguson,
4 Jacob Scudder,
5 John Gulick,
6 Robert Bayles,
7 Mary Berrien,
8 Henry Van Dike,
9 John Gulick, jun.
10 William Gulick,
11 Jacob Gulick,
12 Frederick Cruzer,
13 Cornelius Van Derveer,
14 Samuel Mershon,
15 Job Mershon,
16 William Van Tillburgh,
17 Charles Rule,
18 Daniel Britton,
19 Elias Scudder,
20 Garret Van Derveer,
21 Elias Cowenhoven,
22 William Bickner,
23 John I. Craig,
24 John Reeves,
25 Abraham Voorhees,
26 Job Stockton,
27 Churchill Houston,
28 John Joline,
29 Samuel Cruzer,
30 John Rule,
31 Jacob Van Dike,
32 John S. Nevius,
33 John Blackwell,
34 Henry Gulick, (Ridge)
35 Henry Gulick, (Rocky-Hill)

36 Matthew Patterson,
37 Jacob Quick,
38 John Armstrong,
39 David Baker,
40 Jemima Van Pelt,
41 Joseph Patterson,
42 Willam Bayles,
43 Aaron Longstreet, jun.
44 Elias Baker,
45 Margaret Gulick,
46 Ann Gulick,
47 Sarah Comfort,
48 Mary Gordon,
49 John Cruzer,
50 Gertrude Van Dike,
51 Margaret Blackwell,
52 Isaac Van Dike,
53 James Lake,
54 Jacob H. Van Dike,
55 Rebecca Bayles,
56 John Van Duyn,
57 Anna Hunt,
58 John Van Pelt,
59 Jacob Gulick, (Rocky Hill)
60 Hester R. Scudder,
61 Elizabeth Gulick,
62 John Veghte,
63 John Hollinshead,
64 William Hollinshead,
65 Benjamin Gulick,
66 Ebenezer Stockton,
67 Jerem Van Derveer,
68 Abraham Terhune,
69 Ralph Sansbury,
70 Benjamin Clark.

Early residents of Kingston, Rocky Hill, Princeton, and environs had the opportunity of buying stock in the Kingston Library Company in 1812. The original 70 members paid $1 a year to borrow one of the 284 titles owned when this circulating library first opened in the old academy. Newer books were added around 1852 and the library was still operating as late as1886. This is a page from the "Constitution, Rules, and Catalog of Books and Names of Proprietors." (Courtesy of the Historical Society of Princeton.)

Seven

SPIRITUAL AND SACRED PLACES

This winter scene of the Rocky Hill Dutch Reformed Church and the parsonage on the left predates newer houses along Crescent Avenue that now prevent this view. Prior to its construction, parishioners gathered on Saturdays for Sunday school in a nearby barn or at the old schoolhouse and attended church on Sunday in Harlingen.

A Spiritual Sense of Place

A Presbyterian congregation was organized in the village of Kingston around 1723 and a log cabin church was built around 1730. A second structure, which may have included a schoolroom, was built in 1792. Both of the church buildings are thought to have been in the cemetery where General Washington had briefly conducted his "conference on horseback" after the Battle of Princeton in January 1777. Noteworthy clergymen such as David Brainard and William Tennant preached in Kingston during the Colonial "Great Awakening." A new Presbyterian church was built later in 1852 in Kingston during the "Enlightenment" period.

Ten years before the new Kingston Presbyterian Church was built, residents of Griggstown decided to build a church. They had been attending Dutch Reformed churches in Six Mile Run, Millstone, and Harlingen. In 1842, the First Reformed Protestant Dutch Church of Griggstown was organized. Land for the church was purchased from John and Isaac Gulick and Cornelius Simonson on Canal Road. Fund-raising began immediately. In 1848, property for a parsonage next to the church was purchased. A spiritual movement reached Griggstown in the 1870s and membership nearly doubled by 1876. Many groups within the church were organized, such as the Vanguard Adult Bible Class.

Long before a church in Rocky Hill was built, Sunday school was held in private homes. By 1818, the trustees were permitted to use local buildings on Saturday afternoons for meetings. In 1855, Samuel Brearley, Isaac Vanderveer, and Henry Vreeland were appointed to select a building site and David Mount and Samuel Brearley were to gather design proposals. Land was purchased from Isaac Vanderveer and Thomas J. Skillman for $300 and Brearley and Mount donated land for an adjacent street. The building committee consisted of Samuel Brearley, Thomas J. Sillman, and Westley Morris. Plans by Henry W. Laird of Princeton were approved and the Rocky Hill Reformed Church and furnishings were ready by 1857 at a cost of $4,741.75. Vertical board siding and pointed windows created a "carpenter Gothic" cathedral effect. The building still dominates the town skyline. The parsonage was built the following year.

Parallel to establishing Dutch Reformed churches in Griggstown and Rocky Hill, was the establishment of Trinity Episcopal Church in 1864 in Rocky Hill. Henry McFarlane, of Scottish ancestry, arranged for this small "pattern book" church to be built on part of his mill property on Crescent Avenue. The designs of Richard Upjohn, the architect of New York's Trinity Church, were used. A parish hall was added in 1901. The one hundred-seat church now has Tiffany windows and sponsors various community activities throughout the year.

The Methodist Episcopal movement began in the area after the Civil War, and a church was built in Rocky Hill in 1870 on Princeton Avenue designed to seat 270 people—a sizable number for a small village! In 1878, evangelist Lizzie Sharp came to Rocky Hill and conducted revival meetings in the church. People from Kingston were already attending the church. Miss Sharp was invited to conduct meetings in Kingston too. By 1879, Kingston had also built a Methodist Episcopal church. Both churches struggled to maintain and increase their memberships, but by the early 1900s, the Rocky Hill Church discontinued services and became the Lyric Theater. Kingston's Methodist Church, however, continues to this day.

Evangelical crusades between 1870 and 1920 for temperance, Sabbath-keeping, Sunday schools, and missions caused a rise in church membership. The appeal was based on faith in individual improvement—both spiritual and material. Likewise, the Chautauqua movement encouraged reading and education to rationally address social problems. During this period many libraries and museums were established.

The most recent church built is St. James Catholic Church on Princeton Avenue in Rocky

Hill in 1908. It was built to serve the new Irish and Italian population of the area. Bridget and James Sweeney lived in the Abraham Voorhees house built in the 1840s on Princeton Avenue at the turn of the century (page 86). The Sweeneys donated land nearby for a church and later land for a small cemetery. Prominent members of St. James in the early days were the Scasserras, the O'Malleys, and the Mucillises. Catholic services in the church were discontinued when St. Charles Borromeo was built in Montgomery Township in 1991.

There are a number of family cemetery plots and cemeteries in Griggstown, Rocky Hill, and Kingston. Smaller family graveyards have often not been maintained. Perhaps the oldest gravestones are in Kingston on the former Higgins family plot near Route 27 and Raymond Road. The Kingston Cemetery also dates to the 18th century. The oldest gravestone, dated 1756, is Deborah Leonard. The journalist, Julian Ursin Niemcewicz, wrote an account of Kingston in 1797 mentioning around 20 houses and two inns. Early family names in Kingston were Higgins, Bayles, Lake, Withington, Colby, and Gulick, and these can be found in the cemetery.

The Rocky Hill Cemetery was established in 1858 on 6 acres purchased from Stephen Cromwell for $130. The oldest gravestones reflect the names of early Dutch, French Huguenot, and English settlers: Skillmans, Vanderveers, Voorheeses, Crusers, Vreelands, and many other 19th-century descendants of the original settlers.

The Griggstown Cemetery Association was incorporated in 1924 and includes an old section that was originally on a Veghte farm. In this old section are many of the original settlers of Griggstown. Some of the old names are Hoagland, Staats, Veghte, Elbertson, DeHart, Simonson, Oppie, and VanDoren. In the much older Skillman-Beekman family cemetery are buried Thomas Skillman and Peter Vanderveer. In the Griggstown Cemetery are also 19 unmarked small brown gravestones for Irish laborers who died of the Asiatic cholera while building the Delaware and Raritan Canal. The local Ancient Order of the Hibernains has recently erected a special gravestone monument to these poor souls whose names will never be known.

Before the automobile and improved roads, Rocky Hillians—like everyone else—used horsepower. This photograph was taken in 1890. The Rocky Hill Reformed Church faces what was then Main Street (now Washington Street) on the corner of Church Street (now Reeve Road). The fence is gone, but the church remains the high point of the town's landscape.

This beautifully-maintained Reformed Church "Carpenter Gothic" parsonage was built for $2,300 in 1858 by Joseph Gibson, a Princeton carpenter. Although the porch and the picket fence on Crescent Avenue are now gone, the original wood floors and windows remain.

PICNIC REFORMED SUNDAY SCHOOL

An itinerant photographer probably captured this October 1908 Sunday school picnic group at the Rocky Hill Reformed Church. For a time, Sunday school was held in the old schoolhouse until a Sunday school was added to the back of the church in 1862. Stephen Voorhees wrote a history of the Sunday school in 1878.

Between 1840 and 1862, Episcopal services were held in various residences in Rocky Hill. Henry McFarlane built Woodside on River Road (page 89) and offered his home for services until Trinity Episcopal Church was completed in 1862. This charming pattern-book church on the corner of Crescent Avenue and Park Avenue (which was then Mount Street) seats one hundred parishioners. The donated Tiffany windows enhance its quaintness. Sunday school rooms were added in 1901 and a library was added later.

Palm Sunday during the spring of 1945 was a good time to gather many from the congregation of Trinity Episcopal Church in Rocky Hill for a photograph. The war was over and families were grateful for a return to normal.

St. James Roman Catholic Church in Rocky Hill was built in 1908 to serve the growing Irish and Italian population. Many of these people had taken jobs at the quarry, the Atlantic Terra Cotta factory, the railroad, and Princeton University. A small cemetery lies behind the church on Van Horne Brook. Parishioners have outgrown this small building and now attend either St. Paul's in Princeton or St. Charles Borromeo in Montgomery Township.

The Griggstown Reformed Church is a religious and social cornerstone of the community. It was founded in 1842 by Dutch settlers and with the arrival of Norwegians in the 1920s, membership was again bolstered until the Scandinavians built their Bunker Hill Lutheran Church in 1958. (Courtesy of Shirley Staats Stryker.)

Before 1914, the interior of the Griggstown Reformed Church appeared like this. The classical Greek style is evident both outside and inside of this lovely church on Canal Road. Two organs were pumped by foot power, and kerosene lamps provided the light. (Courtesy of Shirley Staats Stryker.)

The parsonage next to the church in Griggstown was rented by Herbert and Martha (Van Doren) Brush in 1910 and they bought it in the 1940s. This photograph was taken in the 1920s with John and Mary Van Doren, their three sons, Martha Van Doren Brush, and Gertrude Smock. The church repurchased the parsonage in 1974. (Courtesy of Lloyd Van Doren.)

Pictured is the Vanguard Adult Bible class of the Griggstown Reformed Church in 1917. Among the members identified in this photograph are: Charles Cheston, Sadie Wyckoff, Lewis Mosher, Sarah Staats, Herbert Brush, C.A. Hoagland, Dr. A.E. Boice, Mrs. Herbert Brush, Sidney O. Staats, Mrs. A.B. Mosher, Mrs. Ernest Taggart, Mrs. Harvey Boice, Mrs. Fred Wyckoff, Mrs. C.A. Hoagland, Ethel Boice, and C.N. Hoagland.

The newer Kingston Presbyterian Church was built in 1852 on Main Street (now Route 27). The building has Italianate influences with a fine Greek Revival-design cast-iron fence in front. This church, along with the Presbyterian church in nearby Princeton, nurtured the growth of Presbyterianism in the area. By the 19th century, Princeton was at the very heart of Presbyterianism. (Courtesy of the Historical Society of Princeton.)

The interior of the Kingston Presbyterian Church reflects a classic simplicity. The stained-glass windows were added during a renovation and later removed to restore the interior as it was in 1852. (Courtesy of the Kingston Presbyterian Church.)

The Kingston Methodist Episcopal Church was completed in 1879 after Lizzie Sharp's revival meetings inspired a small number of people in town. The Building Committee consisted of Henry R. Hight, Charles B. Robison (a miller), William Bunn, James D. Harris, T.L. Reed, Rev. J.E. Sawn, Charles Green, Charles Stives, M.M.P. Durling, and John Perdun. Lumber for building the church was brought by canal. (Courtesy of the Historical Society of Princeton.)

The interior shows the wonderful organ pipes in the Methodist Episcopal Church now called the Kingston United Methodist Church. The first pastor was Joseph Sawn. Henry R. Hight was superintendent of the Sunday school for over 43 years. He spoke at the 50th anniversary program in 1929. The Building Committee consisted of: Henry R. Hight, Charles B. Robison (a miller), William Bunn, James D. Harris, T.L. Reed, Rev. J.E. Sawn, Charles Green, Charles Stives, M.M.P. Durling, and John Perdun. Lumber for building the church was brought by canal. (Courtesy of the Kingston United Methodist Church.)

Although this photograph of the Kingston Methodist Episcopal Church League is undated, it may have been made at the 50th anniversary celebrations in 1929. (Courtesy of the Historical Society of Princeton.)

This view of Kingston at the cemetery may have been taken around 1913 when the King's Highway was renamed the "Lincoln Highway" (now Route 27). The Kingston Presbyterian Cemetery sits on the hill to the right. It is not difficult to imagine General Washington stopping here on horseback to determine the route for his victorious troops after the Battle of Princeton in 1777. (Courtesy of the Delaware and Raritan Canal Commission.)

VanTilburgh's Inn, the Sign of the Mermaid, was on the corner of the King's Highway opposite what is now called Heathcote Road in Kingston. His final resting place in the Kingston Presbyterian Cemetery shows William Van Tilburgh's death at age 84 in 1804. The tavern was demolished in 1880.

These neglected gravestones on the Jedediah Higgins property near Raymond Road in Kingston are perhaps the only genuine remains of an early settler of the village. Jedediah Higgins built a house on the King's Highway in the early 1700s. John Dalley of Kingston made a map in 1745 that confirms the general location of the Higgins property. (Courtesy of Clem Fiori.)

Scattered throughout the older section of the Rocky Hill Cemetery are the gravestones of many whose legacy in the village during the 19th century still remains apparent. The graves of Abram and Phebe Vanderveer are a reminder of those who came before us. They lived on a 95-acre homestead on Princeton Avenue and were active members of the Dutch Reformed Church. They were close neighbors of Abraham and Abigail (Vanderveer) Voorhees who also lived on Princeton Avenue. (Courtesy of Clem Fiori.)

These unmarked brownstone (red shale) graves of 19 Irish canal workers who perished from Asiatic cholera during the 1831–32 epidemic, are in the Griggstown Cemetery on Canal Road.

Eight

LIFE IN THE VILLAGES

Pictured here are the Smalley family children with their goat cart in Rocky Hill c. 1910. The Smalleys were interested in all forms of transportation! (Courtesy of the Historical Society of Princeton.)

Lifestyles of Neighbors and Friends

Woodrow Wilson called the automobile "a picture of the arrogance of wealth." He made this comment in 1906 while he was president of Princeton University. It was a signal for reform. He went on to become the governor of New Jersey and President of the United States. A political faction, called the Progressives, supported Wilson and urged an end to big business abuses. They also made demands for better education, labor reforms, and aid for the less fortunate.

Victorian America produced a middle class, as ordinary people began to have savings, were better educated, and had a bit more leisure time. Mail orders for everything from suspenders to bungalow-style houses were possible. This was the age of family picnics, country fairs, church suppers, card clubs, parlor pianos, croquet, band concerts, and the soda fountain. A nickel in 1904 bought an ice cream cone, a cup of coffee, a phone call, a shave and a hair cut, or a newspaper. Door-to-door deliveries of meat, milk, coal, produce, and other groceries predate modern supermarkets. Doctors even made house calls by carriage or car to take care of accidents on site, sick patients, or to deliver a baby. It was possible to listen in on your neighbor's conversation by the telephone "party lines" to find out who was ill, whose wedding was planned, or who had died.

The shift from horsepower to gasoline power changed lifestyles completely. Owning a car was both a status symbol and a means of getting around on your own. Well-to-do businessmen and doctors were among the first to own cars, but later, cars became common and could be seen at swimming spots, in parades, and parked in front of houses and businesses. Excursions into the countryside were a popular pastime for those who owned automobiles. For others in larger towns, the trolley enabled them to get around and perhaps find a job farther from the neighborhood. The growth of the railroad network laid the foundation for the growth of suburbs.

The canal communities of Rocky Hill, Kingston, and Griggstown began to seek a different quality of life after the 19th-century commercial boom. As canal and railroad traffic declined in the lower Millstone River Valley, the villages changed focus. Life settled down again with a resurgence of community-oriented activities that provided the people in these crossroads settlements with a renewed sense of place. Itinerant photographers enjoyed depicting everyday events and scenes in the early part of this century, leaving a marvelous record of people and places that are less known.

The workplace, recreational activities, and often a crisis drew people together in common pursuits. Schools, churches, and volunteer organizations provide the framework for the character of these three communities. Names in school rosters, fire departments, church records, cemeteries, and clubs reflect the diversity that developed in the population of these towns.

Athletic teams were formed to provide for the recreational and social needs of young men during their leisure time. Baseball and basketball were the favorite team sports, and the surrounding villages sent teams to play each other. Carl Robbins raised $92 in the 1940s to start a young boys' baseball team and they were permitted to remodel the basement of Voorhees Hall with the help of Linus Gilbert, owner of the quarry. This became their headquarters. The YMCA became active around WW I. Swimming in the canal and the river was a summertime activity enjoyed by all and playing on the frozen canal in the winter was an outlet for young children. Bicycling became a craze. Camping along the canal drew young people from far away. In the summer of 1934, Dr. Acken rented his campground in Griggstown to a group of two hundred German-American youths called "Camp Wille und Macht" (Will and Might).

Occasional tension with boys from the nearby YMCA camp and local complaints about the marching through town were part of this brief episode and the camp closed that August.

Floods and fund-raisers also drew people together for a cause. The Millstone River periodically overflows its banks to cover roads, damage bridges, flood stores and houses, and interrupt daily life. This has not changed since Colonial times. Water in abundance and water shortages meant helping each other out during those times. This spirit of common cause contributed to volunteer activities in the villages for raising money. Plant and flower sales, auctions, clambakes, holiday fairs, shows, and suppers have helped Griggstown, Rocky Hill, and Kingston raise the extra funds needed to maintain their quality of life.

Parades to celebrate and honor those who have served and those who participate in community life have remained a part of town activities. Local businesses continue to support public functions such as parades and milestone events. Doctors, teachers, fire chiefs, and town benefactors are still honored at such events and thus, have become a part of the town's heritage.

The villages have absorbed surges of new residents ever since the Colonial period. The earlier Dutch, Scottish, English, French Huguenot, and African-American residents had established themselves during this time. Newer arrivals often faced language barriers and occasional discrimination. Poor immigrants from Ireland had arrived to build the canal; immigrants from Italy came to work the many quarries in the area and to provide skilled masons for building projects. A few German-Americans also settled in the villages or owned farms. Until the Depression in the 1930s, there were nearby jobs for everyone. The next big wave of newcomers was the arrival of the Norwegians and other Scandinavians who gradually settled permanently in Griggstown between 1926 and WW II. About 50 Norwegian families from Brooklyn bought acre lots off Bunker Hill Road to build small summer bungalows. The Bervens were the first to permanently move in 1929. Sunset Hill development began much the same way. Their musical and poetic talents were personified in John Rutherford, who arrived in 1938 and became known as the "Bard of Norseville." It would not be until the early 1960s that another wave of newcomers arrived. Princeton Ridge development in Rocky Hill drew many new families into the Borough who were mostly professionals and worked out of town. The story of the three villages as portrayed in this book ends in the 1960s.

Old timers will remember the "swimming hole" in the Millstone River in Rocky Hill. In the early 1940s, the Robotti property on the north side of Washington Street was called Robotti Park or Riverside Grove. Louis Robotti worked in the terra cotta factory after he arrived in Rocky Hill in the early 1930s. The family also owned the Gable Tavern on Washington Street between 1934 and 1970. Edna Robotti, a daughter of Louis, ran a store on Washington Street that was a favorite stopover for a cup of coffee or an ice cream cone.

In 1954, Linus R. Gilbert, owner of Kingston Traprock quarry, built a swimming pool for the residents of Rocky Hill, Kingston, and Princeton. It was located behind Trinity church off Park Avenue in Rocky Hill. Blasting at the quarry eventually resulted in serious cracks in the sides of the pool and it was closed in the 1960s. Mr. Gilbert had also, earlier, contributed a youth recreation room in the Voorhees Hall building.

Amy Speinheimer Garrett, wife of Ralph "Cap" Garrett, was probably photographed around the 1920s when the couple moved to 62 Washington Street in Rocky Hill. Ralph worked at the Atlantic Terra Cotta factory and Amy had been a housekeeper before her marriage. They had no children and their home had no running water. When Mrs. Garrett died in 1963, the house was purchased and restored by the Rocky Hill Community Group for their headquarters.

Since 1964, the Rocky Hill Community Group Plant and Flower Sale has been an annual spring fund-raising event. This photograph shows the first sale before the Amy Garrett house was restored. The lady on the left is Vivian Engelbrecht. She and her husband, Robert, were the driving forces who managed the purchase and restoration of the house, which became the community center and the first town library in 1966. (In 1974, a new library was built nearby that is part of the Somerset County system.)

The Atlantic Terra Cotta baseball team posed in 1920. Pictured from left to right are: (front row) Fred White, Mike Kebish, Ray Durling, Wally Volk, Tom Schott, and Wilbur Buchanan; (back row) Harry Newhouse, John Sabo, Bill Volk, Dick Young (manager), Jim McCarthy, Ed Carroll, and "Fat" Lewis. The batboy is unidentified.

The Rocky Hill baseball team played neighboring towns such as Hopewell, Kingston, and Griggstown. The team was organized in the 1920s with 16 members. Irving Robbins is on the right with Barney McClosky next to him.

Bid 'n Buy was an annual event sponsored by the Rocky Hill Community Group as a fund-raiser to support their various activities. This group acts as an organizer for projects in town such as scholarships, maintaining an archive and museum, maintaining the Amy Garrett house, holiday charitable work, and the Independence Day picnic. Bid 'n Buy has been discontinued, but other annual events continue such as the book sale, the plant sale, the July picnic, and a holiday party and tree lighting in December.

Rocky Hill Hook and Ladder Company carnivals were a tradition in town from the 1920s until the 1960s. These were held on the fire company field at the corner of Princeton Avenue and Crescent Avenue. Donors from as far away as New York, New Brunswick, Trenton, and Somerville, as well as local businesses and individuals helped out with this event. (Courtesy of Peggy Harris.)

Irving Robbins was born in Rocky Hill on Montgomery Avenue in 1891 and was a model maker at the terra cotta factory and later a butcher. He helped prepare the decorative terra cotta for the Woolworth building in New York. This photograph dates from 1966. His father, Augustus, was a mechanic at the terra cotta factory, a bridge tender for 50¢ a day, and later a butcher. The Robbins family has lived in town for several generations.

This 1922 photograph of Montgomery Avenue in Rocky Hill facing the Reformed church was the way the street looked when school children attended Washington School on the left side (not pictured). The old Skillman Italianate farmhouse on the far left (page 87) and tenant house (now 3 Montgomery Avenue) can be seen in the center left. This street now leads borough residents to Borough Hall and farther on to the Rocky Hill cemetery.

This charming 1888 scene in Rocky Hill includes, from left to right: brother and sister Frank and Ella Voorhees and Jeannette Griggs. The photograph was taken in the field next to Borough Hall. Jeannette Griggs later married Harry Stryker, who worked for the railroad. Her father was a partner in the Williamson and Griggs general store.

Rocky Hill organized a YMCA group in 1915 following the example of the group established by Herbert Brush in Griggstown. This group of young men pursued a variety of recreational activities, which included basketball games, camping, and staging plays. (Courtesy of Lloyd Van Doren.)

John Van Zandt Griggs owned this Oldsmobile 3280 with black leather seats. It was the first car in Rocky Hill in 1900. By 1905, the song "In My Merry Oldsmobile" was a popular jingle used to sell these cars.

Dr. Malvern Reeve was honored on his 100th birthday in 1965 by the entire town of Rocky Hill. He practiced medicine in the area from 1901 until his retirement in 1959 after earning his M.D. degree from Hahnemann Medical School in 1899. It is said that he delivered three thousand babies and never lost a mother. His office has been moved to a room in the Amy Garrett House. On his 101st birthday in 1966, Church Street was renamed Reeve Road in his honor.

Dr. Abram B. Mosher served the Griggstown and Rocky Hill area by horse and buggy in the late 19th century and practiced medicine for 60 years. His parents were Louis H. Mosher (superintendent of schools) and Matilda Beekman. In 1879, he graduated from the New York University medical school, married Anna Schultz, and moved to a farm on River Road in what was then considered part of Griggstown (now Belle Mead). In 1904, he became one of the first telephone owners in the area. (Courtesy of the Griggstown Historical Society.)

These "bridge beauties" pose all dressed up on the bridge in Griggstown. Perhaps they were a group of teachers from the area. (Courtesy of Virginia Dey Craig.)

Members of the Rightmire family have been living on the Delaware and Raritan Canal in Griggstown for several generations. John Rightmire Jr. was often seen sitting in his carriage with his horse "May" trotting along in front as he traveled along the canal. In this photograph, we see a family outing on the canal. (Courtesy of George Rightmire)

Sledding on a frozen Delaware and Raritan Canal provided Mary Rightmire and her dogs with a way to enjoy winter. The canal water level was lowered during the coldest winter months. Today, the water level remains high to provide water resources to the area. (Courtesy of George Rightmire.)

Bathers in the Delaware and Raritan Canal at Griggstown gather near their automobiles, some still dressed in their Sunday best. Those who owned property on the canal would charge people for parking. The meadow between the river and the canal was a favorite spot for camping, picnics, and enjoying the swimming. (Courtesy of the Griggstown Historical Society.)

The "king-post" swing bridge at Griggstown towards the right in the photograph and a rustic diving board brought summer bathers pleasure in the canal. Some swimmers even braved jumping off the bridge posts. (Courtesy of the Griggstown Historical Society.)

Thomas Arnesen, Pareli Olsen, and Adolph Johansen of Brooklyn, New York, were among the first Norwegian-Americans to purchase lots at $55 an acre from Dr. John B. Acken in Griggstown. In 1925, Norseville was incorporated by the State of New Jersey and the official dedication was held on May 30, 1926. This 1925 photograph shows the founders of Norseville. (Courtesy of Evelyn Peters.)

Peder and Oluf Pedersen built seven bungalows in Norseville. Pictured here in 1928 is one of these with a Model T Ford in front. At first, the Norwegian Americans used their bungalows only during the summer months to find relief from the city heat, but later many of them moved permanently to this rural hamlet. (Courtesy of Esther Olsen.)

Norseville baseball in Griggstown took hold around 1927 when (left to right) Howard Craig; Albert Olsen in the back; and on the grass, Robert Olsen; Virginia Dey; and Sam Bellero began slugging balls. Two in this photograph eventually married. (Courtesy of Virginia Dey Craig.)

Dr. Acken sold more lots in 1927 from his 55-acre farm in Griggstown at $160 an acre. A new section off Bunker Hill Road called Sunset Hill was developed. The Olsens were one of the original families who bought here. Families from other Scandinavian countries joined their friends, and Griggstown still maintains an active Norwegian-American population. (Courtesy of Richard Olsen.)

The whole town comes out to see a new fire truck! Kingston's fire department had just bought a 1958 Ward LaFrance. Armand Petrillo and Earl Mertz carry the banner as the parade turns the corner at Kingston's village center at Laurel Avenue and Main Street (Route 27). Notice the road signs indicating distances to nearby towns and cities. (Courtesy of George Luck Jr.)

Pictured above are ladies in a Kingston card club who took a trip to New York City in the 1950s. From left to right they are: Leah Brindley, Helen McWhorter, Anne Hopfner, Mary Bernard, Sue Rightmire, Eve Potts, Helen Taglioli, Evelyn Mershon, Laura "Lila" Watson, Grace Davall, LouEtta Carrol, and Verna Anderson.

B.S. Peebles grocery store on the corner of Main Street and Laurel Avenue in the 1930s was a favorite place in Kingston to fetch groceries by bicycle. This intersection has changed character considerably today. (Courtesy of Rick Goeke.)

Sometimes Kingston had too much water. This 1929 flood of the Millstone River at the Kingston Roller Mill, shows Billie Thompson, Brazelie Kirby, Len Green, and Nelson Thompson surveying the flood damage from the river. B.C. Kirby was on the Board of the Methodist Episcopal Church and Nelson Thompson was with the owner of the mill. (Courtesy of Rick Goeke.)

Kingston's Main Street has been called the Old Post Road, the King's Highway, the Lincoln Highway, or Route 27. The road has carried travellers, soldiers, the mail, and now commuters north and south between Princeton and New Brunswick. This street scene is of the village center facing the Franklin Township side of Route 27. (Courtesy of Lou Sincak.)

Gen. George Washington traveled through Kingston on the King's Highway in April 1789 to his inauguration as our country's first president. This photograph taken 150 years later in 1939, is a reenactment of President Washington's inaugural trip to New York City. Reminders of the Colonial period, the American Revolution, and George Washington's leadership continue to play a prominent role in historical and preservation activities in the area. (Courtesy of the Historical Society of Princeton.)